Environment, Famine, and Politics in Ethiopia

Environment, Famine, and Politics in Ethiopia

A View from the Village

Alemneh Dejene

Lynne Rienner Publishers ▪ Boulder & London

All photographs are by the author.

Published in the United States of America in 1990 by
Lynne Rienner Publishers, Inc.
1800 30th Street, Boulder, Colorado 80301

and in the United Kingdom by
Lynne Rienner Publishers, Inc.
3 Henrietta Street, Covent Garden, London WC2E 8LU

Library of Congress Cataloging-in-Publication Data
Alemneh Dejene.
  Environment, famine, and politics in Ethiopia: a view from the
  village / by Alemneh Dejene.
  Includes bibliographical references and index.
  ISBN 1-55587-240-9
  1. Land use—Ethiopia. 2. Famine—Ethiopia. 3. Desertification—Ethiopia.
4. Environmental policy—Ethiopia. I. Title.
HD979.A65 1991   90-8816
333.73'0963—dc20   CIP

British Cataloguing in Publication Data
A Cataloguing in Publication record for this book
is available from the British Library.

Printed and bound in the United States of America

The paper used in this publication meets the requirements
of the American National Standard for Permanence of
Paper for Printed Library Materials Z39.48-1984.

To the memory of my father

Contents

Tables and Figures

Tables

Figures

Acknowledgments

It is difficult to acknowledge all those who have assisted me during the three years it took to complete this study. However, I am much obliged to mention the names of a few who have greatly contributed to the project.

The Energy and Environmental Policy Center at the John F. Kennedy School of Government, Harvard University, served as my institutional base and generously supported my research activities. I am thankful to Francisco Szekely, William Hogan, and Henry Lee. I also extend my deep appreciation to Mary Anderson, Peter Woodrow, and Peter Ashton at Harvard University. I thank Allan Hoben, James McCann, Elene Mekonnen, Michael Guillen, and members of the First Church in Cambridge, Massachusetts, for their encouragement. The support of the Rockefeller Foundation was crucial in initiating the study. I am grateful to Robert Herdt who took a special interest in the project.

In Ethiopia, Seyoum Alemayehu (a forester) and Mohamed Ahmed (an agronomist) worked closely with me in the generation of the data. They accompanied me every place that I traveled in both Wollo and the western part of Ethiopia. I was inspired by their love for their country, their sense of responsibility, and their commitment to improving the conditions of the Ethiopian peasantry. Experiencing rural Ethiopia with them is a lifetime memory for which I am grateful.

I am also thankful to Emanuel Haile and Mekonnen Aklog who were part of the research team in Wollo. Dr. Solomon Belete, former commission of planning of Wollo, provided thoughtful comments regarding the methodology of study and the sampling strategy.

The Ministry of Agriculture staff, at all levels, was most cooperative. The former vice minister for natural resource conservation and development, Aklu Girgire, and the present vice minister, Berhanu Debele, were very supportive. Kebede Tato, head of the Community Forestry and Soil Conservation Department, were instrumental in providing support in all the stages of this study. The Land Use and Regulatory Department also contributed to this effort. In particular, I greatly benefited from the insightful suggestions of Dr. K.N.S. Nair in the design of the survey questionnaire.

I am indebted to Bo Goransson, former coordinator of Swedish International Development Authority (SIDA) aid to Ethiopia and advisor to the Ministry of Agriculture, and his wife, Cecilia Backlander, who took a distinct interest in the study and initiated SIDA's support. I extend my appreciation to Workineh Degefu, head of the National Meteorological Service Agency, and Meteke Beyene, head of the Central Statistical Authority, for their support.

A draft of the manuscript was carefully read by Judith Heyer at Oxford University, Goran Hyden at the University of Florida, Hans Hurni at the University of Bern in Switzerland, and Marten Bendz in Sweden. I am most grateful for their comments. The suggestions of the anonymous reviewer were also valuable, and I thank him/her.

Finally, I extend my deep gratitude to the many men and women who hosted us during the fieldwork in Wollo. Their hospitality and kindness are woven into my memory.

Alemneh Dejene

Environment, Famine, and Politics in Ethiopia

Market day in the lowlands of Yeju.

Debersina, Borena.

1

Introduction

The number of people and countries in Africa engulfed by famine has increased at an alarming rate. In the early 1970s, 70 million people were affected by chronic food shortage. This number had surged to 100 million by 1985.[1] Similarly, in the 1970s, two-thirds of the people in Africa lived in countries where food consumption per capita was increasing, whereas in the 1980s only one-fourth of the people lived in such countries.[2] In 1986, 31% of the world's population (1,570 million people), living in forty-nine developing countries, did not have an adequate dietary energy supply for good health and productive work. Thirty-one of these countries were in sub-Saharan Africa.[3] Ethiopia is one such country, and a third of its population suffers from food shortage even in years when there is adequate rainfall.

In the predominantly agrarian societies of Africa, one of the most ominous threats to the food supply is environmental degradation, the deterioration of croplands, grasslands, and forests. In an attempt to counter the rapid decline of Africa's natural resources, the first United Nations Conference on Desertification was held in Nairobi, Kenya, in 1977. The conference emphasized human activity and pressure on the land as a major contributor to the process of desertification.[4] The result of the conference was a plan of action to combat desertification through ecologically appropriate land use and measures to recover degraded lands. According to the United Nations Environmental Program, that plan has failed because the program has no immediate payoff for either developing or donor countries.[5]

Since the 1977 conference, a number of studies have suggested a self-perpetuating cycle of increased human demand on the ecosystem and vulnerability to famine. These studies have, in particular, identified the degradation of natural resources due to human activities as one of Africa's gravest problems in increasing its food supply.[6] As the World Commission on Environment and Development has succinctly stated, "poverty is a major cause and effect of global environmental problems."[7] The World Commission on Environment has popularized the concept of sustainable development that aims to meet the basic needs of the poor without damaging the environment.

Degradation of drylands, commonly referred to as desertification, is the depletion of the renewable resources essential to the basic needs of a population.

1

This process of degradation destroys the ecological support system and greatly contributes to drought, poverty, and famine in Africa.[8] An estimated 4,500 million hectares of land—land that feeds 850 million people (20% of the world's population)—are seriously threatened by desertification. Each year, 21 million hectares lose all of their productive potential. Most of this degraded land (75%) is located in the dry land areas of the world.[9]

The impact of desertification on sub-Saharan Africa is particularly severe, as 85% of all rangeland (542 million hectares), 80% of all rain-fed cropland (114 million hectares), and 30% of all irrigated land (40 million hectares) are at least moderately desertified.[10] Desertified land has sparse vegetative cover and low productivity (generally less than 400 kilograms of dry matter per hectare per year). Desertifed land does not use rainfall efficiently to produce dry matter, and as a result the yields are often poor. This has increased the speculation that desertification may have contributed to the successive droughts in Africa.[11]

Studies show that rainfall in sub-Saharan Africa has continuously decreased since the late 1960s and the impact of each drought has been more severe than the last.[12] The prevalent explanation for drought and desertification emphasizes the global-scale changes in the atmosphere and in the ocean[13] because changes in land surface due to human activity occur at a slower rate than changes due to atmospheric fluctuations.[14] Recently, however, some have argued that both account for the recurrent drought and famine that affect most of sub-Saharan Africa.[15]

In fact, several feedback mechanisms between the earth's surface and the atmosphere have been identified as reinforcing the cycle of drought.[16] One of the most significant mechanisms is the high reflection rate (albedo) of the sun's radiation due to the absence of vegetative cover. This absence, through a complex process, will eventually lead to dryness of the soil and to reduced cloud formation.[17] A second mechanism accounts for the reduction of locally evaporated moisture. Some researchers argue that a great deal of the rain in the Amazon basin, as well as in the tropical inland of Africa, comes from the evaporation of water from the nearby trees and soil, rather than from the distant ocean.[18]

Other researchers have emphatically asserted that the primary reason for the successive African droughts is the excessive human exploitation of natural resources, which exceeds the land's carrying capacity.[19] Carrying capacity is a calculation that estimates the human and animal population an ecosystem can support without being seriously degraded.[20] Carrying capacity, however, is a relative term that varies among and within regions, as well as with the level of technology, and its applicability is limited. Some proponents of this concept (notably Garret Hardin) have aroused controversy because of their single-minded focus on population growth as the primary source of land degradation and their unduly pessimistic assessment of ecological disaster based on the contested premise that sees the earth as an isolated ecosystem with limited renewable resources.[21] Be this as it may, the role of human beings has become increasingly prominent in explaining the process of ecological degradation in Africa. Harold Dregne, for instance, describes desertification as "the impoverishment of the terrestrial ecosystem under the impact of man."[22]

In Ethiopia, there are three predominant human activities invariably identified as contributing to the vicious cycle of environmental degradation, drought, and famine; these are overgrazing, overcultivation, and deforestation. Nowhere is the adverse impact of human activity on the environment so striking as in the famine-ridden areas of the Ethiopian highlands which occupy 44% of the country's 1,251,282 square kilometers (125,128,196 hectares)[23] and which contain 80% of the country's 47 million people[24] and two-thirds of the 77 million ruminants.[25] These highlands, which include over 90% of the cropland and are the center of the nation's economic activity, suffer from massive land degradation due to soil erosion. It is estimated that 1,900 million tons of soil are eroded annually. About 76% of the highlands' 41 million hectares of land has been significantly or seriously eroded, 4% (2 million hectares) has lost its ability to produce food, and only 20% (10 million hectares) has relatively minor problems of erosion. Given this trend, it is projected that 18% of the highlands will be bare rock by the year 2010 and 10 million people will not be able to produce food from the land.[26]

The intensity of drought in these highlands has worsened in the last two decades.[27] Intensive cultivation, overgrazing, deforestation, overpopulation, and the political and economic forces that relate to peasant agriculture have exerted enormous pressure on the ecosystem. These factors have resulted in soil loss, a substantial loss of vegetative cover, and soil compaction, which have severely reduced soil fertility and crop yields. In 1978, a report circulating in the United States embassy in Addis Ababa pointed out that about one billion tons of topsoil were being eroded from the Ethiopian highlands.[28] Although a direct causal relationship between topsoil erosion and famine is difficult to establish, it is plausible that such massive erosion could lead to the eventual collapse of the ecological support system, particularly in times of drought, resulting in widespread famine as witnessed in 1984.

Objective of the Study

Recent studies have suggested that the process of environmental degradation is largely place specific and is greatly influenced by the local socioeconomic and national political forces operating in a particular society.[29] There has been little precedent for a systematic field study such as this that identifies the forces that feed the interaction between environmental degradation and famine at the house-

Figure 1.1 Map of Ethiopia and Its Regions

This study uses the administrative structure of Ethiopia as it existed prior to January 1989.

hold level and critically examines the impact of government policies upon these forces. The Wollo region of Ethiopia, the most devastated by the 1984 famine, provides a classic representation of the vicious spiral that engulfs most peasant households in the Ethiopian highlands (see Figure 1.1). In addition, this study offers a comparison between peasants' views and Ethiopian government policies on major issues such as resettlement, villagization, tree ownership, population and livestock density, and various conservation and famine prevention activities. The findings bring to light the key issues that need to be considered by policymakers in the attempt to arrest the reinforcing cycle between environmental degradation and famine and to attain sustainable development in Ethiopia.

Chapter 2 specifically examines how the existing socioeconomic forces on peasant farmers' management and utilization of cultivated and grazing land affect the rate of land degradation in Ethiopia. The data provide insight into the debate over what are the primary causes of land degradation in the famine-prone Ethiopian highlands and how these problems should be addressed by the appropriate actions of peasants and by government policies.

Some major physical and social indicators of environmental degradation are compared with peasants' perceptions. Chapter 3 analyzes peasants' views of the Ethiopian government's policies concerning conservation activities and identifies the major obstacles to attaining the rehabilitation of degraded land. Famine has differing impacts on households living in the same peasant association or in close proximity to one another. Chapter 4 identifies the factors that have made a difference in reducing the vulnerability of peasant households in times of drought and famine, highlights the lessons peasants attributed to the 1984 famine, and evaluates the effectiveness of Ethiopian government policies to avert future famine in drought-prone regions such as Wollo.

Chapter 5 explores peasants' views toward resettlement in Wollo and the conditions of Wollo peasants who have settled in the relatively fertile southwest regions following the 1984 famine. This chapter assesses the environmental impact of the government's resettlement program in famine-affected Wollo and in relatively resource-endowed settlement areas. It also investigates whether one of the objectives of resettlement—helping famine victims achieve food self-sufficiency in settlement areas—has been attained, as well as the kinds of constraints faced in meeting these objectives.

The final chapter formulates the major policy issue that emerges from the findings of this study. It argues for major policy reform and the enactment of appropriate legislations that would provide incentive for peasant farmers to undertake conservation and rehabilitation activities. This chapter also identifies the technical packages of conservation projects that have made a substantial contribution in restoring ecological balance while maintaining farmers' productivity.

Methodology of the Study

In an attempt at systematic investigation, the study combined two approaches. In Wollo, where a major part of this study was conducted, survey questionnaires and participant observation were used. In the settlement areas (southwestern Ethiopia), a case study approach, with an in-depth study of a few villages and families, was used. The survey questionnaire was designed in Ethiopia and pretested in Dessie, in the Wollo region (see Appendix 1). The administrative units in Ethiopia were, in descending order of size, administrative regions, awrajas, weredas, and peasant associations. Tragically, the new legal administration, enacted as of January 1989, divided Ethiopia into twenty-five administrative regions and five autonomous regions based on ethnic lines. This division has fueled ethnic hostility and posed an unprecedented threat to the unity of the country. In addition, the new administration dissolved wereda as an administrative unit leaving a wide gap between awraja (considerable large unit) and peasant association at the village level. The leaving out of wereda which has been an intermediary unit between awraja and peasant association has made it difficult for the regional administrators to maintain security and administer development projects at the village level.

As of January 1989, Wollo was also divided into two regions: Southern Wollo, whose capital is Dessie, and Northern Wollo, whose capital is Woldeyia. This division is unpopular among the people of Wollo, and in this study—which was completed before the division—Wollo refers to both Southern and Northern Wollo.

Interviews were conducted among randomly selected heads of household in nine of the twelve awrajas and in nineteen of the thirty-seven weredas of the Wollo region (see Figure 1.2). The sample consisted of 230 households from forty-six peasant associations (see Table 1.1). In addition to its name, each peasant association in Wollo has an identification number in each wereda (the peasant associations selected are presented by their identification numbers in Table 1.1). The selection of the peasant associations was done in close consultation with the Ministry of Agriculture, wereda representatives, and extension agents with knowledge of the area. The factors taken into account in stratifying the peasant associations in each wereda were ecological zones, the extent to which peasant associations were affected by the 1984 famine or had serious land degradation, and the extent to which the composition of households and the problems they faced were representative of the wereda. This method of stratification, known as expert sampling, is based on informed opinion and can be used in generating hypotheses.[30] Although expert sampling is not reliable for statistical analysis, it is useful for the purposes of this study.

Five farmers were interviewed in each peasant association. A two-stage nonprobability and probability sampling was used to select the farmers who were interviewed. The first stage nonprobability sampling involved the deliberate

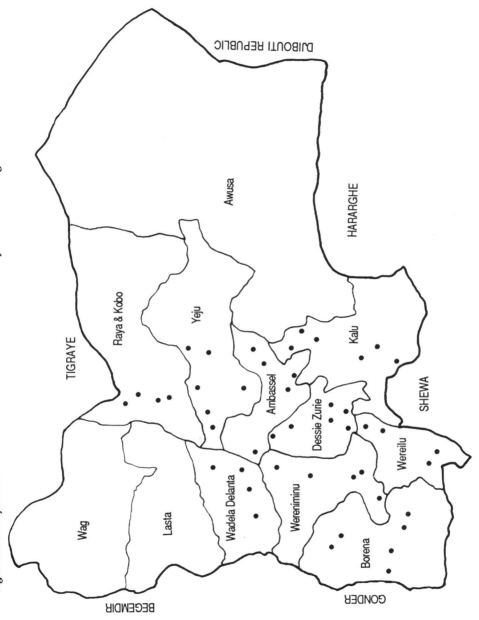

Figure 1.2 Awrajas and Peasant Associations Covered Under the Study in the Wollo Region

decision for five interviewers, including the author, to travel three to ten kilometers in different directions through each peasant association, depending on its area. This dispersal was designed to capture the variations in altitude and soil fertility within each peasant association. Even though peasant associations were stratified by ecological zone, their classification in Wollo is ambiguous. Most peasant associations usually extend from highland to medium altitudes, and in some cases from highland to lowland altitudes, extending over two or three ecological zones. In order to circumvent the uncertainty such a varation might generate, this study considered the predominant ecological zone within each peasant association. Therefore, 26% of the population in the sample were selected from highland areas, 44% from medium altitudes, 28% from lowlands, and 2% from the Alpine *wurch* zones. These figures corresponded roughly to the percentages of the total population living in the four different ecological zones in Wollo.[31]

The next stage in the nonprobability sampling involved not selecting those heads of household whose houses had tin roofs (a sign of wealth) or those who were executive members of the peasant association. Each interviewer selected the first house with a thatched roof that he encountered upon entering the village. If the interviwer could not find the head of the household in the first house, as was often the case, he went to the next house, and so on until he found the head of the household. Before conducting the interview, the interviwer gave an elaborate explanation to gain the farmer's confidence that the study had nothing to do with unpopular government programs, such as resettlement.

A separate questionnaire was designed for the Wollo peasants who were resettled in western Ethiopia as a result of the 1984 famine (see Appendix 2). In this region, the author undertook a case-study approach in which the data were generated by an "in-depth study" of a limited number of farmers and by participant observation. The case-study approach is adaptable to different situations, is easy to carry out, and often leads to deeper insights than large-scale surveys.[32] In addition, the limitations of the questionnaire survey used alone to investigate conditions of the rural poor are well illustrated by what Robert Chambers has called the "pathology of rural surveys." This pathology includes costliness, inefficiency, and often misleading findings in the absence of careful cross-checking and analysis in the attempt to capture and interpret rural realities.[33] Our questionnaire survey was cross-checked by our independent verifications, by a follow-up "in-depth study" of a few informative farmers, and by participant observation while we were conducting the survey. The author also carried out extensive discussions with peasant association leaders, exten-sion agents, and local government officials to obtain relevant information for this study. The other sources for this study were the Ministry of Agriculture's Regional Office for the Wollo, Illubabor, and Keffa regions; the Regional Planning Offices for Northeastern Ethiopia in Dessie and for Southwestern

Methods of data generation: The individual interview, Werebabo, Ambassel.

Methods of data generation: Group participation, Bati, Kalu.

Table 1.1 The Names of Awrajas, Weredas, and Peasant Associations Covered Under the Study

Awraja	Wereda	Number and I.D. Numbers of Peasant Associations		Number of Interviewed Households
1. Borena	Debersina	2	(060, 056)	10
	Kelala	2	(020, 070)	10
	Sayent	2	(01, 02)	10
2. Werehiminu	Legambo	3	(030, 01, 02)	15
	Tenta	1	(08)	5
	Mekedela	1	(012)	5
3. Wereilu	Jamma	2	(013, 024)	10
	Wereilu	2	(019, 017)	10
4. Wadela Delanta	Delanta	4	(040, 02, 017, 032)	20
5. Kalu	Bati	3	(014, 04, 07)	15
	Eseyegola	3	(06, 07, 02)	15
6. Raya & Kobo	Kobo	4	(08, 03, 01, 011)	20
7. Yeju	Habru	3	(018, 038, 01)	15
	Gubalafto	3	(030, 016, 013)	15
8. Ambassel	Tehulederie	2	(010, 012)	10
	Werebabo	2	(012, 013)	10
	Ambassel	1	(034)	5
9. Dessie Zurie	Kutaber	2	(014, 012)	10
	Dessie Zurie	4	(02, 021, 025, 027)	20
Total	19	46		230

Ethiopia in Jima; and the Relief and Rehabilitation Commission in Dessie and Addis Ababa.

Duration of the Study

The field investigation was undertaken from the last week of October, 1987, to the first week of April, 1988. Nearly five months of this period were spent in Wollo and the rest of the time in Illubabor and Keffa, visiting resettlement sites and speaking with the settlers from Wollo. The total distance covered during this study was about 15,000 kilometers, of which 10,000 were in Wollo. The journey to settlement areas started from northern Ethiopia at Raya & Kobo Awraja in Wollo (bordering the Tigraye region) and ended at the western tip of Ethiopia in Gambela Awraja, close to the Sudanese border. Additional field work was also undertaken between October, 1988, and March, 1989, in both Wollo and the settlement areas in western Ethiopia. The total distance covered by car during this period was about 25,000 kilometers. This does not include travel within peasant associations, which was accomplished mostly on foot and, in a few cases, by mule (in Wollo, the roads leading to peasant associations are impenetrable by car).

Limitations on the Study

Large-scale surveys, although appropriate for some studies, were neither feasible for this independent one-man study nor the best method of obtaining reliable information on its major concerns. As a policy research, this study attempts to highlight peasant's perceptions of some key government policies that influence their survival and the management of natural resources. Hence, the approach taken here, as explained by the sampling strategy, is not intended to generate statistically reliable output based on rigorous empirical research. However, it does generate some hypotheses and provides insights into some of the research issues under investigation.

This field survey was undertaken at a time when many areas of Wollo were experiencing major crop failures caused by the shortage of rain during the main planting season in 1987 (*meher* season). Acknowledging the prevailing drought conditions, the government declared a food emergency situation in many parts of Wollo. Relief operations were underway in some of the weredas and peasant associations covered by the study. The drought conditions may have influenced peasants' responses to questions such as whether they had some reserve food at the time or whether they had any assets with which to buy food.

At the time of the study, Wollo was gripped by the hysteria of resettlement (see Chapter 5). Extension agents and party officials were promoting (the term often used was "agitating") the virtues of resettlement, which the peasantry resisted strongly. The farmers were restrained from expressing their views candidly on environmental degradation (Chapter 3). In fact, they were initially apprehensive about why they had been selected for the interviews. Their reactions were understandable, given that it was precisely information regarding degradation that was sought by government officials to determine who should be drafted for the unpopular resettlement program. Thus, we had to reassure the farmers constantly that we were in no way involved with the resettlement program. Judging from their responses, we succeeded in gaining the confidence of the majority of the farmers. Still, it is likely that some remained skeptical.

Suffice it to say, an understanding of this situation is crucial to an examination of the findings of this study.

The Setting

Located in northeastern Ethiopia, Wollo borders the Tigraye region to the north, the Republic of Djibouti and the Hararghe region to the east, the Gojam and Gonder regions to the west, and the northern Shewa region to the south (see Figure 1.1). Wollo has a spectacular landscape: its endless hills and valleys, each one more scenic than the other, are dazzling sights. Wollo has a population of 4,075,959, of which 94% live in rural areas.[34] The largest town in Wollo is Dessie, the capital city of the region, with a population of 68,848. The two other towns, each with a population of 16,000, are Kombolcha (Kalu Awraja), located 23 kilometers south of Dessie, and Woldiya, located about 100 kilometers north of Dessie.[35] The most notable urban enterprises in the region are the soft drink industry in Dessie and the textile and meat industries in Kombolcha.

Wollo is an historic region and a source of great pride to Ethiopia. The oldest remains of humankind, the famous three million-year-old fossil "Lucy," was found in this region. Wollo is the home of two of the oldest churches in Christendom, Lalibela (carved out of solid rock), and Gishen Mariam (Saint Mary), under which a part of the cross on which Jesus was crucified is believed to be buried. The Muslims of this region also proudly recite the heroic battles that Mohammed the "left hander" fought in Wollo during Islam's expansion in Ethiopia. It is also a region recurrently ravaged by famine—about five famine years in this century alone. The most brutal in scope and intensity was that of 1984, which led to the expansion of relief centers in every region of Wollo, an expansion previously unknown in Wollo's history. Through the extensive television coverage they received in 1984, the relief centers at Bati and Korem highlighted the tragedy of famine in this region.

Wollo is also unique in that, in a land marred by ethnic and religious hostilities, the Amhares, the Tigres, and the Oromos (the main ethnic groups in the region) live harmoniously together, often married to one another, despite their differences. Wollo is predominantly Muslim, yet most Muslims also indicate that they are ethnically Amhares, who in most regions are Christian. With respect to religious and ethnic harmony, Wollo is an exemplary region from which the rest of Ethiopia has a great deal to learn.

The character and the spirit of Wollo peasants are equally impressive. Nearly every Wollo peasant experienced the two worst famines in this century— one in 1973/74 and one in 1984/85. The scourge of famine neither subdued the peasants nor haunts them incessantly. They certainly have not forgotten the famine conditions, yet they do not live with it every day. Most peasants interviewed in this study were neither optimistic enough to say that famine would not strike again (as indicated by 13%), nor pessimistic enough to say that famine would recur (as indicated by 27%). The majority of the peasants (60%) left this judgment to God and were striving for better days and a better future.

This attitude does not suggest that these peasants were totally fatalistic and unable to take their destiny into their own hands—an argument often heard by party officials in enforcing unpopular policies such as resettlement and villagization. The peasants' attitudes towards the future should rather be understood to reflect the outlook in a region where both Christianity and Islam are deeply rooted.

Nearly two-thirds of the 8.2 million hectares of land in Wollo is very hilly.[36] The outstanding features of this region are its rugged topography, majestic mountains, and steep escarpments. These mountains and gorges extend, with varying elevations, from northern Shewa to the southern part of Tigraye, dissecting Wollo roughly into a western and eastern catchment. The western catchment includes some of the highest mountain areas in western Wollo, particularly Dessie Zurie, Wereilu, Werehiminu, Borena, and Wadela Delanta awrajas; the streams from these mountains carry enormous amounts of soil to the Beshilo River, a major tributary of the Nile, which passes through most of these awrajas. The eastern catchment consists of the highlands of Ambassel, Kalu, and parts of Yeju, which drain their contents into the Awash River. The mountains of the eastern catchment rise and fall like huge waves and finally merge with the semiarid lowlands where the nomadic Afar tribes are concentrated.

There are five major ecological zones—Alpine, highland, medium altitude, lowland, and arid land (*berha*). Extension agents use altitude to determine ecological zones, while farmers consider the type of cereal grown, which for the most part is significantly related to ecological zone. In the Alpine zone (3,200 meters or more above sea level), only barley is grown. The major crops of the highland area (2,300 to 3,200 meters above sea level) are barley, wheat, oats, horse beans, field peas, and lentils. In the medium altitude zone (1,500 to 2,300 meters), teff, wheat, sorghum, chick-peas, vetch, and niger seed (*noug* in Amharic) are the major crops. In the lowland zone (500 to 1,500 meters), mainly sorghum, maize, chick-peas, and sesame seed are cultivated. Land below 500 meters is usually the sparsely populated nomadic territory. Major crops are cultivated during the *meher* season, which is the principal rainy season extending from late June to early September. Most of the land (80% to 90%) is used for cultivation during the *meher*. Little land is reserved for cultivation during the *belg* season, the short rainy season that occurs mainly in March and April.

Wollo has two distinct types of farmland. The first is land around the homestead, where the house is built (called *guaro*), and the second is farmstead (called *ersha*). The major annual crops for home consumption and some of the perennial crops, such as coffee, are grown on the *guaro*. Farmers consider their *guaros* to be their most productive and fertile plots. Being close to the house, the *guaro* receives more of the natural inputs such as ashes and dung than does the farmstead, which is further away. As a result, crops grown in the *guaro* have a much better chance of survival in times of drought.

Neither the 1975 radical rural land proclamation, which abolished tenancy, nor the government "Marxist" rhetoric of social transformation[37] has so fundamentally threatened this farming system as has the government's national villagization program. Launched in 1985, the program views scattered homesteads as a major obstacle to rural development and requires peasants to move into new villages that the government agents consider to be suitable for development. Villagization attaches small importance to the *guaro* and allocates little land for such purposes. This shift in focus fundamentally alters the peasants' farming system, which has served as a risk-averting mechanism in times of drought as well as in helping to maintain the independent character of the peasantry (the peasants' views on villagization, the impact of villagization on the environment, and its prospects will be examined in Chapter 6). At the time of this study, only 2% of the farmers had moved into new villages in Wollo, one of the lowest figures as compared to many regions in Ethiopia and far below the government's projections.

Land fragmentation is a common feature in Wollo. A farmer usually cultivates two or more crops on various plots that are often located in different zones. Of the farmers sampled, each had an average of four different plots outside his homestead. On the whole, the literature on Ethiopia sees land fragmentation as a vice of peasant agriculture. However, field investigation revealed that the issue to consider is the number and the location of the land parcels a peasant owns rather than land fragmentation per se. Among farmers who own two or three plots, this ingenious scheme of cultivating different crops on plots located in different ecological zones serves as a risk-averting mechanism in times of drought and possibly even helps reduce the incidence of erosion.

Since the 1975 Agrarian Reform, individual farmers have been organized into peasant associations, which are autonomous grassroots organizations. To increase the bargaining power of peasants and to take advantage of the economy of scale in agriculture and enterprise, three to ten peasant associations can link to form service cooperatives. Peasant associations and service cooperatives, in principle, are to be converted stage-by-stage into producer cooperatives through which land will be communally owned and the produce distributed based on labor contribution. In Wollo, there were 1,194 peasant associations consisting of 659,768 heads of household, and 250 producer cooperatives with 34,757 members.38 Individual farmers, with less than 1.5 hectares of land within the peasant associations, represented the predominant mode of farming, and only 4% of the farming population was organized into producer cooperatives.

As in most other regions, individual farmers cultivated 95% of the land.

In spite of heavy-handed promotion by the government, collective farming (under producer cooperatives) made little gain in Wollo, and the overwhelming number (95%) of peasants interviewed wished to remain individual farmers. The strong sentiment expressed against the producer cooperative movement in Wollo seemed to be typical of most areas of the Ethiopian highlands, whereas it has been observed in the highly politicized Arsi region that 75% of interviewed farmers still wished to remain smallholders.[39]

Ministry of Agriculture extension agents with special responsibilities for organizing producer cooperatives admitted that membership in producer cooperatives was declining in Wollo. The government was secretive on this issue and it was difficult to find an exact figure for those who had left producer cooperatives. Yet, discussions with peasant association leaders clearly revealed that more members were abandoning producer cooperatives, except in a few areas where the availability of irrigation lured peasants into membership.

Wollo has been the testing ground for the Ethiopian government's policy of "food self-sufficiency." Of the twelve awrajas, only Borena and Wereilu were considered to be cereal surplus-producing areas. With nearly 10% of Ethiopia's population, events in Wollo, particularly in times of famine, inevitably affect the rest of Ethiopia. Wollo is also strategically important since it links Ethiopia to the port city of Assab to the east and to the other famine-ridden regions of Tigraye and Eriteria to the north. Hence, averting the process of environmental degradation and restoring the ecological balance in Wollo would have an important implication for the rest of the Ethiopian highlands.

More donor and relief agencies were operating in Wollo than in any other region of Ethiopia. These included the Swedish International Development Authority; the Italian Government Development Assistance; the Ethiopian Red Cross funded by the German, the Japanese, and the Swedish Red Cross; Oxfam; Care; World Vision; Save the Children; and other church-affiliated agencies. Most of the representatives of these agencies expressed their deep interest in Wollo and hoped to continue their assistance. A great deal of money has been spent by these agencies in Wollo in the name of development, but their contribution to arresting environmental degradation and rehabilitating degraded lands at the village level has not been significant. One notable exception is the Red Cross-funded Upper Mille and Cheleka Catchment Disaster Prevention Program (which will be discussed in Chapter 6).

To be sure, donor agencies face serious difficulties in working through the bureaucracy of the Ethiopian government. However, there is also a genuine lack of information about the relevant project components that could assist in controlling the forces that fuel environmental degradation and vulnerability to famine at the household level. Through a case study of Wollo, this study attempts to promote an understanding of both the technical and policy constraints under which peasant farming operates at the village level. This understanding could assist in the formulation of appropriate technical packages and support policies and legislation that could lead to a more effective peasant participation in conservation and rehabilitation activities.

Notes

1. *Famine: A Man Made Disaster?* A Report for the Independent Commission on International Humanitarian Issues, New York: Vintage Books, 1985, p. 26.

2. *The Challenge of Hunger in Africa: A Call to Action*, Washington, D.C.: The World Bank, 1988, p. 3.

3. Robert Kates, et al., *The Hunger Report: Update 1989*, The Alan Shawn Feinstein World Hunger Program, Brown University, p3.

4. United Nations Conference on Desertification, *Desertification: Its Causes and Consequences*, Nairobi: Pergamon Press, 1977.

5. *World Resources 1988-89*, World Resource Institute, New York: Basic Books, p. 217.

6. Lloyd Timberlake, *Africa in Crisis: The Causes, the Cures of Environmental Crisis*, Washington, D.C.: Earthscan, 1985. See also: Lester Brown and Edward Wolf, *Reversing Africa's Decline*, World Watch Paper 65, Washington, D.C.: World Watch Institute, 1985; Asit K. Biswas, *Land Use in Africa*, Vol. 3, No. 4, October 1986, pp. 247-60; Michael Glantz, *Droughts and Hunger in Africa: Denying Famine a Future*, Cambridge University Press, 1987.

7. The World Commission on Environment and Development, *Our Common Future*, Oxford: Oxford University Press, p. 3. See also: M. S. Swaminathan and S. K. Sinha, *Global Aspects of Food Production*, Oxford: Tycooly International, 1986.

8. Mostafa K. Tolba, "Desertification in Africa," *Land Use Policy*, Vol. 3, No. 4, 1986, p. 260. See also: World Resource Institute, *World Resources 1988-89*, pp. 215-31.

9. Mostafa K. Tolba, "Desertification in Africa," *Land Use Policy*, Vol. 3, No. 4, 1986, p. 260. See also: Daniel Stiles and Ross Brennan, "The Food Crisis and Environmental Conservation in Africa," *Food Policy*, Vol. 11, No. 4, pp. 298-310.

10. Stiles and Brennan, "The Food Crisis."

11. Henri Houerou and Hubert Gillet. "Conservation Versus Desertization in Africa Arid Lands," in *Conservation Biology: The Science of Scarcity and Diversity*, Michael E. Soule, editor, Sunderland, Mass.: Sineauer Associates, 1986, pp. 446-47.

12. Sharon E. Nicholson, "Sub-Saharan Rainfall 1981-84," *Journal of Climate and Applied Meteorology*, Vol. 24, 1985, pp. 1388-91. See also: A. V. Todorov, "Sahel: The Changing Rainfall Regimes and the 'Normals' Used for Assessment," *Journal of Climate and Applied Meteorology*, Vol. 24, No. 2, 1985, pp. 97-107.

13. M. Kanamitsu and T. N. Krishnamurti, "Northern Summer Tropical Circulations During Drought and Normal Rainfall Months," *Monthly Weather Review*, Vol. 106, No. 3, 1978, pp. 331-347.

14. E. M. Rasmusson, 1987, "Global Climate Change and Variability: Effects on Drought and Desertification in Africa," in Michael H. Glantz, *Drought and Hunger in Africa: Denying Famine a Future*, Cambridge University Press, 1987, pp. 1-20.

15. Sharon E. Nicholson, "Climate, Drought, and Famine in Africa," in Art Hansen and Della E. McMillan, *Food in Sub-Saharan Africa*, Boulder, Colo.: Lynne Rienner Publishers, 1986, pp. 107-28. See also: J. G. Charney, "Dynamics of Deserts and Droughts in the Sahel," *Quarterly Journal of the Royal Meteorological Society*, Vol. 101, 1975, pp. 193-202; J. Otterman, 1974, "Baring High-Albedo Soils and Overgrazing," *Science*, Vol. 186, pp. 531-33, 1974; Michael H. Glantz, *Desertification: Environmental Degradation in and Around Arid Lands*, Boulder, Colo.: Westview Press, 1977.

16. F. Kenneth Hare, *Climate Variations, Drought and Desertification*, No. 653, Geneva, Switzerland: World Meteorological Organization (WMO), 1985.

17. Charney, "Dynamics of Deserts and Droughts."

18. Hare, *Climate Variations*, pp. 20-24. See also: Lester R. Brown, et al., *State of the World 1985*, New York: Norton, pp. 11-12.

19. Garret Hardin, "The Tragedy of the Commons," *Science*, 163, 1968, pp. 1243-1248.

20. The World Bank, *Desertification in the Sahelian and Sudanian Zones of West Africa*, Washington D.C.: The World Bank, 1985, pp. 11-12.

21. "A Tough-Minded Ecologist Comes to Defense of Malthus," *The New York Times*, Tuesday, June 30, 1987, p. C3.

22. Harold E. Dregne, "Aridity and Land Degradation," *Environment*, Vol. 27, No. 8, October 1985, p. 19.

23. Central Statistical Authority, *Facts and Figures*, Addis Ababa, 1987, p. 1.

24. Central Statistical Authority, *Population Situation in Ethiopia—Past, Present, and Future*, Population Studies Series No. 1, Addis Ababa, March 1988, p. 10.

25. Ministry of Agriculture, *Ethiopia: Livestock Sub Sector Review*, Prepared by Australian Agricultural Consulting Management Company, February 1984, p. 12.

26. M. Constable and Members of the Ethiopian Highland Reclamation Study, *The Degradation of Resources and an Evaluation of Actions to Combat It*, Working Paper 19, Ministry of Agriculture, Addis Ababa, December 1984, pp. 23-48.

27. Workineh Degefu, "Some Aspects of Meteorological Drought in Ethiopia," in Glantz, *Drought and Hunger*, pp. 23-36; Tesfaye Haile, "Climatic Variability and Surface Feedback Mechanisms in Relation to the Sahelo-Ethiopian Droughts," Reading: University of Reading, Masters Thesis, 1986.

28. Brown and Wolf, *Reversing Africa's Decline*, p. 7.

29. Brian Spooner and H. S. Mann, *Desertification and Development: Dryland Ecology in Social Perspective*, London: Academic Press, 1982. See also: Piers Blaikie, *The Political Economy of Soil Erosion in Developing Countries*, New York: Longman Development Studies, 1985; David Anderson and Richard Grove, *Conservation in Africa: People, Policies and Practice*, Cambridge: Cambridge University Press, 1987; Michael J. Watts, "Social Theory and Environmental Degradation," in *Desert Development: Man and Technology in Sparselands*, edited by Yehuda Gradus, D. Reidel Publishing Company, 1985, pp. 14-32; Peter D. Little and Michael M. Horowitz, *Lands at Risks in the Third World: Local Level Perspectives*, Boulder, Colo.: Westview Press, 1987.

30. Dan P. Warwick and Charles A. Linger, *The Sample Survey: Theory and Practice*, New York: McGraw Hill Company, 1975, pp. 72-74.

31. There is no single accepted figure for the number of people who live in different ecological zones in Wollo. The Ministry of Agriculture, for example, estimates those who live in lowland zones to be no less than 30%, while the Regional Planning Office

for North Eastern Ethiopia estimates 11%. After discussions with the Ministry of Agriculture staff in Dessie and Dr. Solomon Belete, the former Head of the Regional Planning Office in Dessie, I have selected the figures used in this survey. Both offices consider the figures used in the survey to be fair in the absence of an accurate figure.

32. Micheal M. Cernea and Benjamin Tepping, *A System for Monitoring and Evaluating Agricultural Extension Projects*, Washington D.C., World Bank Staff Working Paper No. 272, The World Bank, pp. 59-61, See also: Michael M. Cernea, *Putting People First: Sociological Variables in Rural Development*, Oxford University Press, 1985, pp. 3-19.

33. Robert Chambers: *Rural Development: Putting the Last First*, New York: Longman, 1983, pp. 49-64.

34. Central Statistical Authority, *Population Situation in Ethiopia*, p. 10.

35. Central Statistical Authority, *Population of Weredas, and Towns, by Sex and Average Household Size*, Addis Ababa, Census Supplement 1, December 1985, pp. 128-133.

36. Central Statistical Authority, *Area by Region, Awraja, and Wereda*, Statistical Bulletin 49, Addis Ababa, 1986, p. 30.

37. On the nature of the 1974 Ethiopian revolution the following are useful readings: Christopher Clapham, *Transformation and Continuity in Revolutionary Ethiopia*, Cambridge: Cambridge University Press, 1988. Edmond Keller, *Revolutionary Ethiopia: From Empire to a People's Republic*, Bloomington, Indiana: Indiana University Press, 1988. John Harbeson, *The Ethiopian Transformation: The Quest for the Post-Imperial State*, Boulder, Colorado: Westview Press, 1988. Marina Ottaway, "State Power Consolidation in Ethiopia" in Edmund J. Keller & Donald Rothchild, *Afro-Marxist Regimes: Ideology and Public Policy*, Boulder, Colorado: Lynne Rienner Publishers, 1987. Dessalegn Rahmato, *Agrarian Reform in Ethiopia*, Uppsala, Scandinavian Institute of African Studies, 1984.

38. Central Statistical Authority, *Facts and Figures*, Addis Ababa, 1987, pp. 35-36.

39. Alemneh Dejene, *Peasant, Agrarian Socialism, and Rural Development in Ethiopia*, Boulder, Colorado: Westview Press, 1987.

2

The Core of Environmental Degradation: A Grassroots Perspective

Land Use and Management

The peasant agricultural sector comprises 90% of the Ethiopian population and contributes to 50% of the gross domestic product and 90% of the nation's export earnings.[1] In a society so dominated by peasant agriculture, survival is inextricably linked to the exploitation of the land. No area of the country is free from the imminent threat of land degradation. The most severe threat to peasant production is in the highlands that include the Wollo region.

The collapse of peasant farm production that ends in famine in Ethiopia has been outlined in a World Bank study done by Kenneth Newcombe:[2] (1) the rate of forest harvest for fuel, construction, and other needs exceeds supply; (2) timber is sold to other rural and urban areas and there is increased reliance on dung and crop residue for fuel; mineral retention and recycling of the soil is reduced; (3) all tree cover is removed; dung and crop residue become a major source of fuel; the destruction of soil nutrients accelerates and crop yield declines; (4) dung is the only source of fuel and a major source of cash; topsoil is depleted and erosion is dramatic; (5) soil organic content needed for production disappears; collapse in peasant farming usually triggered by drought that could previously be tolerated; this leads to the final stage of massive starvation and emigration to urban areas.

The major cause of land degradation in Ethiopia is soil erosion. The erosion in the Ethiopian highlands, amounting to nearly one billion tons of soil lost each year, is due not to natural causes but primarily to human activities, particularly overgrazing, overcultivation and deforestation. Soil, a delicate renewable natural resource, becomes degraded when it loses its productivity. The water absorptive capacity of soil and the quality of the plant root zone (known as the A-horizon) are two important elements in maintaining soil productivity. In the case of the Ethiopian highlands, soil depth is a reliable indicator of these two elements of soil productivity as well as the extent of erosion. The minimum soil depth required for food crops is 10 centimeters. About 12% of the land in the Ethiopian highlands (which includes part of the Wollo region) has a soil depth

A classic site of severely degraded land in the Ethiopian highlands, Gishen, Ambassel.

A gully expanding on farmland, Gubalafto, Yeju.

of less than 10 centimeters, while one-third has a soil depth of less than 5 centimeters.[3]

While the figures on the amount of erosion are staggering, the major causes remain unclear. The Universal Soil Loss Equation (USLE) is the most widely used method of estimating soil erosion. The basic components of the USLE are the rainfall erosivity factor (R), soil erodability factor (K), slope length factor (L), topographic factor (LS), crop management factor (C), and supporting conservation practice factor (P).[4] Hans Hurni pioneered the application of a simplified model of the USLE to the Ethiopian highlands that stressed rainfall erosivity (R), soil erodability (K), slope length (L) and gradient (S), and land cover (C), which includes vegetative cover, ploughing, and farming practices. From experimental plots, he found that the extent of erosion is significantly related to vegetative cover on the soil.[5]

In specifically examining soil loss due to lack of land cover, the C value for cropland is between 10% and 25% (depending on the kind of crops), for degraded grassland is 5%, and for dense forest is 0.1%.[6] Hence, cropland has the highest amount of soil loss while it is negligible on forest land. In addition, Hurni found that the ratio by which soil loss rates exceed soil formation rates is four to ten times greater on cultivated land than on grassland, depending on agroclimatic zones.[7] Hurni also estimated the total soil loss due to the absence of vegetative cover for different land use systems in Ethiopia using experimental plots and the estimated amount of land under crops, grazing, and forest, as indicated by the Ethiopian Highland Reclamation Study (see Table 2.1).

Table 2.1 shows the enormous variation in soil loss depending on land use

Table 2.1 Estimated Rates of Soil Loss on Slopes in Ethiopia Dependent on the Land Cover

Land Cover Type	Area in Percentage	Estimated Soil Loss	
		tons/ha/year	tons/year
Cropland	13.1	42	672,000,000
Perennial crops	1.7	8	17,000,000
Grazing land	51.0	5	312,000,000
Currently unproductive	3.8	70	325,000,000
Currently uncultivable	18.7	5	114,000,000
Forests	3.6	1	4,000,000
Wood and Bushland	8.1	5	49,000,000
Total loss	100.0	12	1,493,000,000

Source: Hans Hurni, 1986[8]

and suggests that the amount of vegetative cover on the soil is the most important factor in ascertaining the extent of soil erosion. Severe erosion takes place on cropland, which has no vegetative cover during ploughing and the early stages of plant growth. Cropland, which covers 16.3 million hectares, is thus the largest contributor to soil erosion in Ethiopia.[9] Vegetative cover, through a slower infiltration, adds water absorptive capacity and organic content to soil, thereby enriching it. The amount of vegetative cover is greatly affected by the utilization of land for cropping, livestock grazing, and forestry activities to meet the dietary requirements of peasant farmers.

Livestock Density

With twenty-seven million cattle (of which five to six million are oxen), twenty-four million sheep, eighteen million goats, seven million equines, and one million camels, Ethiopia has one of the largest livestock populations in Africa.[10] Between 70% to 80% of these livestock are found in the highlands, and Wollo, with over five million livestock, is one of the regions with high density. The peasant sector, using and managing nearly 95% of the land in Ethiopia, is characterized by subsistence farming, which involves simultaneous crop cultivation and livestock rearing on family farms. Oxen are the only source of traction power. Cattle byproducts such as milk and meat are both consumed and sold. Small flocks of sheep and goats are sources of cash for the majority of highland peasantry. As a result, Ethiopian agriculture is often referred to as mixed farming.

There are some misconceptions about the role of livestock in Ethiopian agriculture. First, livestock are generally regarded as a major activity of the lowland areas. However, one study has shown that the highlands, which have high population density also have high livestock density, indicating that live-stock are important.[11] Second, it is often argued that peasants in the highlands are mainly interested in maintaining large herds for traction power.[12] However, the statistical correlation between human and livestock populations was higher (R=0.86) than the correlation between the intensity of cultivated land (proportion of land under cultivation to total land area) and livestock population (R=0.70).[13] These statistics indicate that livestock not only provide draft power, but are also significant assets that the highland peasant would like to accumulate. Of the farmers sampled in this study, 82% of those who lived in the highland and medium altitude zones (over 1,500 meters above sea level) indicated that they faced serious shortage of grazing land, as opposed to the 18% of those who lived in the lowlands. In spite of this shortage, nearly all of the sampled farmers indicated a desire to maximize their stock. They did not feel that reducing the size of their herds would help overcome the shortage of grazing. The peasant most often identified as a well-to-do farmer in a community had more livestock than land. In addition, the 1975 Agrarian Reform that nationalized all rural lands encouraged ownership of livestock among peasant farmers, since livestock are the only resource that belongs to individual peasant families.

The third misconception involves classifying Ethiopian agriculture as "mixed farming," which implies that crop production and livestock rearing are complementary. Clearly, livestock provide crucial support to cropping in terms of traction, manure, and transportation. However, it is estimated that 70% of the cattle and 71% of the sheep and goats graze on individual holdings of between 0.1 to 2 hectares of land (individual farmers have 4.7 cattle, 3.8 sheep and 3.5 cattle per holding on the average).[14] Thus, as the population increases, so does the livestock density, resulting in an intense demand for grazing land. This has created a condition where livestock grazing and crop farming frequently compete for the same land. This competition is fueled by the norms of a social system that regard the possession of many livestock as a sign of wealth.

A perceptive work on the nature of this competition and its adverse effect on vegetative cover is K. N. N. S. Nair's *Ethiopia: Economic Analysis of Land Use*. Nair's observations are grounded in fieldwork, and are not impressionistic. His approach in examining livestock density and grazing patterns has led him to conclude that the presence of livestock is the "culprit" in land degradation in highland Ethiopia, and that all other factors are secondary.[15] Through a more systematic examination of grazing patterns, this study does provide empirical support for Nair's argument that livestock play a significant role in the loss of vegetative cover. However, this study does not have adequate evidence to conclude that livestock are the major factor in land degradation.

Grazing Patterns

One of the notable features of the Ethiopian highlands are the hills and valleys, which are a pleasure to view and a challenge to field research. To uncover the causes of land degradation, this study aimed to find a pattern in the locations of the homestead, the major cropping plot, and the grazing area for different seasons of the year. Generally, a farmer's house was located on the upper section of a slope or on the top of a hill. This was the case among 60% of the farmers in the sample, while 20% lived on the lower slope of the hill. Cropping, as indicated by 70% of the farmers, usually took place in the valleys, plains, and on the lower slopes. Those who reported that their major crop areas were on an upper slope totaled only 8%, and those who utilized the middle slope totaled 22%.

Farmers were asked whether their livestock grazed in different areas during the rainy and dry seasons. This question is fundamental to understanding whether livestock and cropping are in competition with one another, and to what extent these activities contribute to the loss of vegetative cover. An overwhelming number of respondents (80%) indicated that grazing occured in different areas during the rainy and dry seasons: only 20% of the respondents, living mostly in the lowlands, reported that their livestock grazed in the same area during both seasons, often in the communally owned valleys. Table 2.2 presents the location of grazing land during the rainy season, for those whose livestock grazed in different areas.

Regardless of the ecological zone, the planting of major crops occurs during the primary rainy season, known as the *meher* season. Table 2.2 shows that the majority of respondents (57%) grazed their cattle on slopes in the rainy season, since the valleys and plains are drenched with water, making grazing difficult. Moreover, it is during the rainy season that farmers plough the relatively fertile valleys and plains in preparation for planting. Yet a considerable number of respondents (37%) used the valleys, plains, and croplands for grazing lands that are better suited than the slopes for cultivation. Thus, it is conceivable that livestock are in direct competition with crop farming for the best land, even at a time when land is urgently sought for cultivation.

The findings in Table 2.2 have two important implications regarding livestock's direct contribution to soil erosion. Most of the livestock grazed on the slopes during the rainy season, a period when most erosion occurs. Slope gradient greatly increases the velocity and the volume of runoff. Hans Hurni's study indicates that 10% of the soil is irreversibly lost by downstream runoff from the highlands. Thus, livestock grazing has a great impact on the loss of vegetative cover and degradation of the slope at a time when the worst form of erosion is taking place. Second, large numbers of livestock were grazing in the fertile valleys at a time when the land is too wet, and soil structure and organic matter can be damaged. (This valley grazing may have to do with the government's promotion of hillside closures to rehabilitate degraded areas after the 1984 famine; this topic will be discussed in detail below.)

It is widely believed that land degradation in the highlands (soil erosion in particular) is mainly caused by cultivation. According to the Hans Hurni study, soil loss on cultivated land is estimated to be four to ten times higher than on grazing land, and 80% of the recorded annual soil loss occurs in the month of ploughing and in the first month after planting the crops.[16] Without questioning the

Table 2.2 The Location of Livestock Grazing During the Rainy Season

Location of Livestock Grazing	Number of Respondents	Percentage of Respondents
Plateau (top of the hill)	11	6
Slope (upper, middle & lower)	101	57
Valley	23	13
Plain	26	15
Cropland	15	9
Total	176	100

Livestock grazing on cropland, Habru, Yeju.

Dust erosion from trampling by goats, the lowlands of Bati.

Table 2.3 The Location of Livestock Grazing During the Dry Season

Location of Livestock Grazing	Number of Respondents	Percentage of Respondents
Slope (upper, middle & lower)	8	4
Valley	5	3
Plain	18	10
Cropland	145	83
Total	176	100

validity of Hurni's assessment, this study points out that ploughing alone does not fully explain the level of erosion during the short rainy season. The Ethiopian Highland Reclamation Study stresses that the condition of the land prior to planting during the short rainy season (*belg*, which comes right after the long dry season) or during the first period of growth is important in averting erosion. As the findings from Table 2.3 show, the condition of croplands is greatly affected by livestock. Eighty-three percent of the population grazed their livestock on cropland during the long dry season, which lasts about six months. Immediately after a harvest, croplands, be they on the slopes, valleys, or plains, are left for uncontrolled grazing. Livestock roam everywhere, feeding on crop residue and creating enormous stress on the most fertile agricultural lands. This grazing results in soil crusting, which reduces infiltration and the ability of the soil to absorb moisture. Consequently, the soil on the valuable cropland becomes vulnerable to erosion during the rainy season. Thus, the role of livestock and grazing patterns in creating the nearly barren condition of the soil prior to and during the short rainy season (*belg*) and resulting in severe erosion is greatly underestimated.

Ownership of Grazing Land

One of the most influential works written on the impact of livestock on the environment is Garret Hardin's "The Tragedy of the Commons." In this article, Hardin emphasized the fact that livestock are an important asset, and therefore individual herders will maximize their herd size on communal grazing land.[17] Hence, the only restriction on an individual's amount of livestock is the carrying capacity of the land. There are some case studies, however, that point out that groups can successfully manage communal resources.[18] The tragedy in Ethiopia is not so much a result of the maximization of individual interest on communal property, but rather of communal and private land being left open for grazing. Hardin's arguments contain some truths but are still far from encompassing the whole truth in Ethiopia.

Table 2.4 Type of Ownership of Grazing Land
During the Rainy and Dry Seasons

| | Percentage of Respondents by Season | |
Type of Ownership	Rainy Season	Dry Season
Individual Plot	28	16
Communal Land Belonging To		
Peasant Association	63	71
Both Individual and Communal Land	9	13
Total	100	100

Since the 1975 Agrarian Reform, all rural land, both grazing and cropland, is under the jurisdiction of peasant associations, which distribute it among their members. The Agrarian Reform has brought relative equity to landholding with regard to croplands. However, it has left the issue surrounding livestock ownership and grazing land untouched. Table 2.4 shows that the dominant grazing place in both the rainy and dry seasons in Wollo was still the communal land, owned by peasant associations.

More farmers used their individual plots for grazing during the rainy season (28%) than during the dry season (16%). These data were consistent with other findings of this study that indicated an acute shortage of grazing land among 50% of the respondents in the rainy season, as opposed to 33% in the dry season.

Two distinct groups of farmers were observed among those who relied on their own plots for grazing during the rainy season. The first group included those who lived in a peasant association where there was a hillside closure and the slopes were no longer available for grazing. Most of the farmers in this group bitterly complained that they were facing chronic shortage of livestock feed because of hillside closures. An example of such a farmer lived in Dessie Zurie Awraja, Dessie Zurie Wereda, in the Tebasit peasant association, which extends from 3,000 to 3,300 meters above sea level. This sixty-four-year-old farmer's house faced the forbidden hill, about 150 meters away. The farmer had one ox, one cow and one heifer, ten sheep, and two equines. His sheep, an important source of cash income, used to roam freely on the hill. Now, his livestock mostly browsed around the homestead. He admitted that he sometimes took a quick walk in the evening to fetch some grass and vegetation from the hill to bring home for his livestock.

The second group included farmers who reported severe shortages of grazing land mainly due to the small size of the peasant association and the large human and livestock populations. An example of the latter was the Ambamariam peasant association (012) in Werehiminu Awraja, Mekedela Wereda, which encompasses 800 hectares and 814 members, and where the average cultivable land is under one-half of a hectare. Most of the respondents in this peasant association brought hay and grass to their homesteads for livestock. They were experiencing serious shortages of grazing land, particularly in the rainy season, when the plots were urgently needed for cultivation.

In Wollo, as in many parts of the Ethiopian highlands, ownership of grazing land is transient and depends upon the season, except for the area around a farmer's homestead. Private plots used for cropping during the rainy season are thrown open for public grazing once the harvesting of crops is completed. Each member of the peasant association will have unrestricted access to other members' plots during the dry season, except to those plots around the homesteads. Consequently, the problem in Wollo is not so much the "tragedy of the commons" but rather the fact that neither communal nor private lands are properly managed for grazing. Improper land management is the primary factor in the loss of vegetative cover. The loss of vegetative cover is in turn a major cause of soil erosion and of the loss of productive land in Ethiopia.

Cultivation and Human Pressure on the Land

There are two distinct cultivation practices in Ethiopia. One farming system uses oxen to plough (annual crops) while the other uses manual hoe cultivation (for perennial root crops). The northern highlands are dominated by oxen ploughing, which is believed to have been brought by the Semitic people who migrated across the Red Sea about three thousand years ago.[19]

In this century, two phenomena may be observed with regard to cultivation practices due to increasing human and livestock pressure in the northern Ethiopian highlands. The first involves "outward" expansion, in which new or fallow land is brought under cultivation. This expansion continues until all the productive land is used effectively. Most of the northern highlands have passed this stage and are now in the second phase, known as "inward" expansion, which involves cultivating the same land more intensively and frequently every year without fallow. Nearly all the farmers in the sample were aware that they were cultivating the land more often than they used to. Only 5% of the farmers interviewed practiced fallowing, which is an indigenous means of maintaining soil fertility.

Most farmers in this survey pointed to overcultivation due to shortage of land as a major factor in reducing soil fertility. This consensus is similar to the findings of the highland reclamation study. [20] These peasant perceptions are supported by the data, which indicate that 60% of erosion in the highlands occurs in areas (referred to as low potential cereal zones) that are cropped intensively and have little forest cover.[21] Although cropland constitutes 13% of the area in the highlands, 45% of the total erosion on the slopes, amounting to 1,493 million tons per year, comes from cropland. Average soil loss on cropland is 42 tons per hectare per year, which means an annual reduction of 1 to 2% in soil fertility.[22] As pointed out earlier, livestock also play a major role as they graze on most of the cropland right after harvest.

One-third of the Ethiopian highlands has a slope exceeding 30% gradient[23] and is not suited for intensive cultivation as currently practiced; yet most cropping in Wollo takes place on the slope. Lacking proper management, farming practices on the slope worsen the problem of soil erosion. The vulnerability to erosion arises not so much from the traditional Ethiopian plough (*maresha*), which has minimal tillage, but more from the amount of ploughing during field preparation (three to six times depending on a crop), the absence of contour ploughing, terracing, or perennial crops, which grow throughout the year, and the lack of manure or crop residue to increase soil fertility.

The absence of vegetative cover on cropland is a major reason for the large quantity of soil loss and the small amount of organic content in the soil. Without proper conservation methods and farming practices, crop cultivation on the slopes will continue to have a devastating impact on productive land. In Wollo there were widespread gullies close to the croplands and a considerable number of farmers in the sample were cultivating slopes exceeding 30% gradient. The number of farmers who were applying manure was insignificant. Manure in the form of dung was either a major or the only source of fuel in most parts of Wollo, where chemical fertilizers were unknown to most peasant farmers, except those

Farmland full of stones due to intensive cultivation and soil erosion, Dessie Zurie.

in producer cooperatives.

In sum, intensive cultivation, lack of appropriate conservation and agronomic practices to maintain vegetative cover, and a decline in the traditional use of manure have resulted in the severe depletion of land resources in the central highlands. These problems are acutely obvious in the highlands of Wollo. The only exceptions are the relatively fertile southern and southwestern highlands, which were being threatened by the massive resettlement scheme (to be discussed below).

A major factor contributing to overcultivation is the explosive population growth in Ethiopia. There are no reliable population figures prior to 1984, when the first systematic national census was carried out. The 1984 census estimated Ethiopia's population to be 42.2 million, compared to the estimated figure of 34.6 million in use at that time. The nations's Ten Year Plan, 1984/85-1993/94, approved by the government, used the 34.6 million figure for its projections on such key issues as education, health, and other social services.

The 1984 census has created serious doubts about the population figures and growth-rate estimates prior to 1984. Using the 1984 census data, population projections were reconstructed for the years 1950-2035, assuming no fertility control.

Table 2.5 reveals that the population growth rate in Ethiopia is staggering. At the time of the worst famine in 1984, the number of mouths Ethiopia had to

Table 2.5 Reconstructed Estimates of Past Population, Projected Population, and Population Growth Rate

Year	Population (in millions)	Annual Growth Rate (%)
1950	19.2	2.0
1955	21.2	2.1
1960	23.5	2.2
1965	26.3	2.3
1970	29.5	2.3
1975	33.1	2.6
1980	37.7	2.8
1984	42.2	2.8
1990	49.9	2.8
1995	57.9	3.0
2000	67.8	3.2
2005	80.1	3.3
2010	95.5	3.5
2015	114.5	3.7
2020	138.2	3.8
2025	167.7	3.9
2030	204.7	4.0
2035	251.2	4.1

Source: Central Statistical Office, 1988[24]

feed was more than twice that in 1950. Without a major fertility decline, Ethiopia will have to feed a population nearly three times greater in the year 2015. These are frightening figures to consider since the land cannot support even the present population. Moreover, in times of famine the needs of such a large population will make relief operations immensely difficult.

An important feature of Ethiopia's population is its majority of young people. Of the 47.3 million people living in Ethiopia in 1988, 47% of the population (or 22 million people) were under the age of fifteen years.[25] These figures signify a high dependency burden on the working-age population. Every working person supports himself and an additional 105 dependents. Moreover, these young people have to be educated, but have little chance of being absorbed into the labor market. They will also contribute to the expanding population in the immediate future.

The disturbing trend in Ethiopia's population size and age structure at the national level was also observed in this study. The average size of a household in this sample was 5.8 people, including children and other relatives who were dependent on the household food resources. The 1984 census shows the average household size for Wollo as 4.1, but it does not explain who is included as members of a household. This survey indicated that the average number of children (dead or alive) begotten by the head of the household in all families was six. An average of 4.4 of these children lived. An average of 3.2 of them were under the age of eighteen, and could not, therefore, own land in the peasant associations.

This study investigated the impact of the number of dependent children in a household on vulnerability to famine. Households that reported not having enough food to last them until the next harvest—between three and six months from the time of the interview—were considered "vulnerable to famine." Dependent children in this study were those under the age of eighteen, since membership in the peasant association is granted at that age.

There was no statistical relationship between household vulnerability to famine and the number of dependent children under the age of seventeen. An examination of the households that did not have adequate food until the next harvest (referred to as "vulnerable to famine") showed that of the twelve households with no dependents, only two were "vulnerable to famine," and six of the total thirty households with one dependent child were "vulnerable to famine" (see Figure 2.1). Only a small number of households with six or more dependent children are shown as "vulnerable to famine" because few households in the sample exceeded six dependent children.

However, the negative impact of a large number of children under the age of 18 on the availability of food reserve may be seen in two peasant associations (013, 024) in Jamma Wereda. Jamma Wereda (Wereilu Awraja) has some of the most extensive flat and relatively fertile land in Wollo. Jamma, usually a food surplus-producing wereda, was severely affected by the 1987 drought.

When this survey was conducted, members of these peasant associations were receiving food assistance. Farmers in these peasant associations had an average land size of 1.2 hectares. Most of them had a pair of oxen and none were without livestock.

In the first peasant association (013), two heads of household, with families of two and zero dependents, respectively, reported having enough food for six months. Of the three households with no reserve food, relying on relief, the first had a family of six with four dependent children; the second, a family of five with two dependent children; and the third, a family of four with two dependent children. In the second peasant association (024), a similar pattern was observed. Two respondents with no reserve food had eight and nine members in their families, including six dependent children in each household. Among those who had reported having enough food were two families, each with seven members, including three dependent children, and another household with three members, of whom one was dependent. These limited findings suggest that, all factors being equal, larger families with more dependent children were more likely to be vulnerable in times of famine.

The growth of the child-bearing population is another factor that exacerbates the population problem in Ethiopia. The age structure statistics of Ethiopia's population (1988) indicated that 24% of the female population and 22% of the male population were between the ages of fifteen and twenty-nine, a prime age in fertility.[26] The findings from this survey, however, showed that age, particularly among men, did not often influence the tendency to have more children. Of the 17% of the farmers in the sample who were sixty-years-old or older, the majority (68%) had one or two children under age five.

One example of such a farmer was a sixty-year-old Muslim man in the Kendo peasant association (02), Legambo Wereda, Werehiminu Awraja. This farmer lived in the Alpine zone (*wurch*) at an altitude of 3,550 meters—the highest altitude encountered during the field research. He was married five times. From two marriages he had thirteen children, of whom six had died. Two of the deaths were due to the 1984 famine. He had six children by his present wife, who was forty years old. Of the eight people in this household, three were children under the age of five, and two are between the ages of five and seventeen. This farmer cultivated barley on one hectare of his land and used all of his harvest for family consumption. Yet he reported having no reserve food and being on the brink of starvation.

Like most of the farmers with many dependent children, this farmer from Werehiminu did not believe that having had fewer children would have improved his condition. On the contrary, he relied a great deal on the assistance of his children in both the planting and harvesting seasons. The repeated statement made in the development literature that children are a major means of security during old age is true; at the same time, dependents are an intense strain on the meager resources of rural households in Ethiopia.

The Impact of Population Growth on Land Size and Fertility

The impact of the burgeoning population on farm size, particularly when there is limited potential to expand land within a peasant association, is a serious problem in Ethiopia, and Wollo is no exception. In fact, some predict an absolute land shortage in the highlands of Ethiopia by the year 2015. Even if a strict population policy is adopted now, it will have a lag period of twenty to twenty-five years before population growth is significantly reduced. Hence, it is estimated that individual holdings in the highlands will average 0.6 hectare per household by 2015.[27] This is below the 1 hectare of land that is essential to sustaining both human and livestock needs. The question to be addressed is whether the data generated from the study support these assessments. If so, what are the implications for environmental degradation and famine?

The average total landholding of farmers in this study was 1.5 hectares, and the average cultivated area was 1.4 hectares in Wollo. The above finding is nearly identical to the 1984 Agricultural Survey, which revealed the average total land size to be 1.57 hectares, and the cultivable land to be 1.42 hectares.[28] These figures on average land size for the whole region nevertheless conceal the substantial differences one finds between awrajas, weredas, and ecological zones.

The availability of cultivable land in Borena, Werehiminu, and Wereilu awrajas in western Wollo is diminishing. According to respondents, the average cultivated land in western Wollo was 1 hectare, and in Yeju and Ambassel (in northern Wollo) is 1.1 and 1.3 hectares, respectively. In these awrajas, most of the farmers cultivated all of their holdings and no longer practiced fallowing. Moreover, an increasing amount of marginal land on the upper slope and escarpment was being brought under cultivation in most of the highlands. Hoe cultivation was prevalent on such steep slopes and on summits, as oxen ploughing becomes nearly impossible at a slope gradient of well over 50%. In Ambassel, one is astonished at the sight of men, suspended by rope, farming the steepest escarpment. In search of new land, some peasants were moving closer to the mountain slopes, thus resulting in the emergence of what Dessalegn Rahmato has called "mountain people."[29] Following the Agrarian Reform, the size of individual holdings decreased through redistribution (new members join the peasant associations at the age of eighteen), as indicated by 59% of the respondents. There was also no mechanism to bring new land under cultivation by the peasant association. Uncontrolled population growth causes the law of diminishing returns to take hold for most peasant associations, particularly in the fertile highland and medium altitude zones. Survival will mean intensive cultivation of the most marginal land at the expense of environmental protection.

Ecological zone is an important factor influencing the size of the peasant association, the size of landholdings in the peasant association, and the population density that affects soil degradation. The average size of a peasant association was 1,362 hectares in the highlands, 1,516 hectares in the medium altitude, and 2,263 hectares in the lowland zone, indicating a statistically significant relationship between the size of the peasant association and the ecological zone. Similarly, the overwhelming majority of those plots under one hectare in size were located in the highland and the medium altitude zones, while those with a land size of two or more hectares were concentrated in the lowlands.

When the relationship between land size and vulnerability to famine was examined, an interesting observation came to light. In the highland and medium altitude zones, considerable numbers of the respondents with less than one hectare of land were more vulnerable to famine than those with over one hectare. However, in the lowland zones of Kobo, Bati, and Werebabo weredas, most of the interviewed farmers had an average of two hectares and still were seriously threatened by famine. The highlands have relatively greater biomass production (which contributes to maintaining soil fertility) than the lowland, due to higher rainfall. Hence, the chances of total crop failure in times of drought is most likely to be reduced in the highland areas.

However, because of high population growth, the size of individually owned plots is shrinking in the relatively fertile highland and medium altitudes. This diminution will lead to intensive cultivation, which will inevitably result in a loss of soil fertility. In the absence of modern techniques for enriching the soil, and with dung being increasingly converted into a source of fuel, the reduction of soil fertility is imminent. Thus, diminishing land size will lead to reduced soil fertility and, subsequently, to a decline in both the soil's capacity to produce food and its resistance to drought conditions.

The significant relationship observed in the Arsi region between large membership in the relatively fertile highland and medium altitude zones and considerably smaller numbers in lowland zones was not observed in Wollo.[30] The average number of households in a peasant association in the highlands was 613, in medium altitude 526, and in the lowland zone 680. This distribution may be due in part to the stratification of peasant associations in the lowland zones, which has concentrated in areas that were deeply affected by famine. These lowland zones with high population densities were also more vulnerable to famine, as indicated in Table 2.6.

Table 2.6 indicates a statistically significant relationship between ecological zone and vulnerability to famine. In addition to having less rainfall and biomass production, the lowland areas in this study also had larger household sizes than those in the highland and medium altitudes. The average household size in the lowlands was 6.3, while those in the highland and medium altitudes were 5.5 and 5.8, respectively. Kobo Wereda is one of the lowland areas that was devastated by both the 1973 and 1984 famines, and where the greatest number of the respondents (eighteen out of twenty farmers interviewed) were vulnerable to famine. The peasant associations in the sample had an average total size of 3,456 hectares, 1,560 of which were cultivated, and the average number of members in the peasant associations was 1,064. The average household size among the respondents in Kobo Wereda was 6.4. A further investigation of the relationship between family size and vulnerability to famine revealed that the size of a family can have an adverse impact on household food availability.

This study questions the applicability of Ester Boserup's central thesis that greater population density has led to innovation in agriculture and advancement in technology.[31] Boserup's thesis has held true for Europe, North America, the Soviet Union, and parts of Asia, all of which had the resource base for industrialization. Many of these countries were also supported by historical circumstances, such as colonialism. Such conditions are hardly noticeable in the most densely populated highlands of Ethiopia and other sub-Saharan African countries that are severely affected by recurrent famine. For example, a regional study in Tanzania showed that an increase in population density resulted in the shrinking of cultivable land, severe land degradation, and a decrease in food production.[32] Hence, population density in the famine-prone regions contributes to the vicious cycle of environmental degradation and famine instead of creating the technological conditions that could increase the food supply.

Table 2.6 Relationship Between Ecological Zones and Vulnerability to Famine

Ecological Zones	Vulnerable	Not vulnerable	Number of Cases
Highland	17%	83%	59
Medium altitude	22%	78%	100
Lowland	72%	28%	65
Alpine (wurch)	33%	67%	6

Note: Chi square significant at 0.001 level

Deforestation

Figures are unlikely to capture the level of deforestation in the highlands of Ethiopia. Even to the eye of the casual observer, the bare mountains and hills along the main road from Addis Ababa to Asmara testify to the extent of deforestation in Ethiopia. Gullies running from the tops to the bottoms of the hills are a common sight in Wollo and a painful reminder of the difference forests and vegetative cover make in preventing such massive erosion.

In the western highlands of Wollo, Borena, Werehiminu, Dessie Zurie, and Wadela Delanta awrajas, one witnesses accelerating surface runoff, a catastrophic consequence of the absence of forests. In these highlands, the topsoil is swept away by streams and fed to the Beshilo River. Similarly, a massive amount of soil is carried away from the northern highlands of Wollo

(Lasta and Raya Kobo awrajas) by the Tekezae River, another major tributary of the Nile. The genesis of the impoverishment of Ethiopia's soil begins in these bare highlands.

Trees and forest vegetation, which once covered the Ethiopian highlands, have the remarkable capacity to reduce soil erosion: the canopies of trees minimize the impact of rainfall, leaves and bark litter replenish organic matter in the soil, and roots keep soil intact, preventing it from being detached easily. Trees also serve as windbreaks, preventing the soil from being carried away by wind. Studies on the Amazon rain forest indicate that nearly three-fourths of the rain there reenters the atmosphere either in the form of evaporation from the trees and soil or through transpiration from the plants. As a result, forests are referred to by ecologists as "rain machines."[33] A study by the National Academy of Science shows that evaporation also accounts for one-third to two-thirds of rain formation in the semiarid regions of the Sahel.[34] With massive deforestation such as that seen in Wollo, the amount of moisture recycled into the atmosphere after it rains is substantially diminished while runoff increases. Thus, the disappearance of forest contributes to the disruption of the equilibrium that affects the rainfall pattern.

At present, the forest reserves in Ethiopia are estimated to be under 3%, and about 100,000 hectares of forests are lost annually.[35] It is commonly reported that at the turn of the century, Ethiopia had 40% of its forest reserves intact. However, further discussion on this subject with Ministry of Agriculture staff in Ethiopia and researchers such as Hans Hurni and K.N.N.S. Nair suggests this assessment is likely to be wrong. In a country whose civilization extends back three thousand years, deforestation north of the Nile River is most unlikely to have occurred in the last century alone. It is true that deforestation may have accelerated by as much as 40% in the last century, with the result that the nation's forest reserves have shrunk to the present level. The rapid loss of forest since the turn of this century has more to do with the substantial increase in both human and livestock populations, which has put more demand on forest land, than a mere increase in fuelwood consumption.

According to farmers, the major causes of the disappearance of forests were the increase in land cultivation; human consumption for fuel, housing, and other necessities; livestock grazing; and settlements. A number of the respondents indicated that all of the above activities, to a varying degree, contributed to the vanishing of forests in their communities. Yet, at the same time, most of the farmers interviewed considered the need to expand cultivated land for cropping as the primary cause.

Clearly, the clearing of forests for annual crops for family consumption and livestock rearing has accelerated to keep up with the dramatic surge in population. Shifting cultivation, a harmless practice with regard to soil fertility when the human and livestock populations were smaller, overwhelmed the land capacity at the turn of this century. Prolonged fallowing could no longer be sustained (only 5% of the farmers in this study were practicing fallowing). As a result, forests and woody vegetation could no longer regenerate or reoccupy, as they had in previous centuries. Forests, which promote ecological stability, quickly gave way to less desirable vegetation and grasses; their presence, which still minimizes erosion, has substantially decreased as well. This change is due to intense grazing in both the rainy and dry seasons, as indicated in Tables 2.2 and 2.3.

The government of Ethiopia is aware of the extent of the deforestation, but the prescription to deal with this problem has given more power to government agencies and less to peasant farmers and their institutions. As a result, the great deal of human and capital resources committed to afforestation projects had only marginal impact.

The 1975 Agrarian Reform abolished private ownership of forests. Forests covering more than 80 hectares were placed under the jurisdiction of the government State Forest Development Department while smaller plots were to be administered by the peasant associations. These newly formed associations were suddenly entrusted with power without having any guidelines for managing forest resources. In addition, they had neither the institutional capacity nor the manpower to manage forest resources. The government admitted that a far greater number of forests were abused by the public in the years following the 1975 proclamation than before. In 1980, another proclamation announced the creation of an autonomous agency, the Forestry and Wildlife Conservation and Development Authority, within the Ministry of Agriculture which had the authority to administer the conservation and management of the nation's forests and wildlife. This agency was brought under the Natural Resource Development Main Department with the reorganization of the Ministry of Agriculture in 1985. The creation and strengthening of forestry institutions are useful, but their efforts are severely constrained by the absence of a coherent national forestry policy to deal with the issues of ownership in Ethiopia.

Government afforestation activities are undertaken by the Community Forestry and Soil Conservation Department and the State Forest Development Department, both of which fall under the Natural Resource Development Main Department of the Ministry of Agriculture. Afforestation programs run by the Community Forestry and Soil Conservation Department are undertaken on degraded lands, hillsides, mountains, and community forests within peasant associations, and are usually supported by the Food for Work Program. Tree planting on state forest land is also largely supported by the Food for Work Program. The Community Forestry and Soil Conservation Department assists peasant associations in the establishment of community forests, a major afforestation activity at the village level.

The main outside support for afforestation programs comes from the World Food Program, the Federal Republic of Germany, and the Swedish International Development Authority. Most of the tree planting activities are undertaken in famine-prone regions, particularly in Wollo. Seedlings are planted in the peasant associations' community and state forests, and are under the supervision of the Community Forestry and Soil Conservation Department. The number of seedlings planted between 1982 and 1987 was 51,458,957 (an average of 7.4 million seedlings per year), by the State Forest Development Department, 67,861,997 (an average of 9.7 million seedlings per year), and by the Community Forestry and Soil Conservation Department, 48,333,000 (an average of 6.9 million seedlings) per year.[36]

An examination of the yearly figures, shows that the amount of seedlings planted after 1985, following the 1984 famine, was nearly three to five times greater under all schemes than it was prior to 1985. However, the figures on the number of seedlings planted should be taken cautiously. Even if such massive numbers were planted, the survival rate must have been very low, since we did not see millions of small trees during visits to the plantation sites. As one of the Ministry of Agriculture officials put it, "if all the reported seedlings have been planted and a third of them have survived, Wollo could become a tree exporting region."

The actual afforestation activities in 1986 in Wollo exemplify the unreliability of the figures on seedlings planted and their survival rate as given by the Ministry of Agriculture Zonal Office in Dessie (see Table 2.7). Table 2.7 indicates that a total of 30,640,426 seedlings were planted in Wollo in 1986. The seedlings planted were *Eucalyptus globus* and *grandus*, *Juniperus procera* (Amharic name "thid"), *Olea africana* (Amharic name "weyera"), and *Acacia*. Although figures on the types of trees planted were unavailable, extension agents pointed out *Eucalyptus* and *Juniperus procera* accounted for the majority of seedlings that were distributed for planting. The average survival rate of all seedlings planted in 1986 was estimated to be 38.7%. This means that 11,845,587 would have survived. This survival rate cannot be taken seriously. There are several potential causes for this exaggeration. First, the survival rate is reported once a year—usually in December before the start of the long dry season, and conditions can change drastically between then and the next year. Second, the figures given for one year are not verified the following year; this assumes that plants continue to survive after the first year, when in fact they have died. Third, there is a serious shortage of labor for checking the survival rate, which consequently has become the guesswork of overworked agents who are obliged to report a figure at the end of the year.

Irrespective of the debate over the reliability of the figures for seedlings planted and their survival rate, serious afforestation efforts were undertaken in Wollo following the 1984 famine. However, two important factors, one related to the other, have made these efforts largely ineffective. Afforestation is seen mainly as the planting of trees, and the equally important factor of the ownership, management, and utilization of these trees is given little consideration. In addition, there is no coherent national forestry policy in Ethiopia. Hence, the severe

Table 2.7 Seedlings Planted in Wollo in 1986

| | Number of Seedlings Planted By | | |
Awrajas	Community Forest and Soil Conservation Department	State Forest Development Department	Community Forest of Peasant Association
1. Wereilu	1,862,959	—	1,928
2. Werehiminu	2,850,418	2,153,636	904,871
3. Borena	1,519,842	—	440,220
4. Kalu	3,002,110	—	910,076
5. Dessie Zurie	1,926,581	1,397,493	1,795,050
6. Wadela Delanta	374,259	441,107	1,387,110
7. Ambassel	2,461,576	895,248	241,360
8. Yeju	1,659,919	1,147,283	366,679
9. Raya Kobo	348,776	407,852	—
10. Lasta	624,234	705,831	2,300
11. Wage	368,723	374,101	57,960
12. Awusa	—	10,924	—
Total	16,999,397	7,533,475	6,107,554

Source: Ministry of Agriculture Zonal Office in Dessie, Wollo

limitations of afforestation programs in Wollo, as well as in the rest of Ethiopia, arise from the political and socioeconomic forces under which they operate.

Policy Constraints in Planting Trees at the Village Level

Dwindling forest resources brought a corresponding reduction in the application of dung to enrich the soil's organic content. In Wollo, as in many parts of the Ethiopian highlands, dung is increasingly being used as a primary source of fuel. Hence, increasing the wood supply is an important means by which to arrest land degradation and soil erosion.

The demand for wood to meet basic needs exceeds the available supply in Ethiopia. It is estimated that the annual demand for fuelwood exceeds the supply by nearly two times: 42 million cubic meters as opposed to 24 million.[37] Again, the most important factor in influencing the demand for wood is population size. Given the present trend of over 2.9% annual population growth in Ethiopia, the outlook for adjusting this imbalance, at least on the demand side, is dismal. The question then becomes whether this imbalance can be adjusted by increasing the wood supply.

The wood supply in Ethiopia comes from trees around the homesteads and farm land; natural woodland within and outside the community; community forests; and state forests (large-scale plantations). Peasant households, in principle, have access to all of the above sources of fuelwood, except for state forests, which belong to the government. Trees around the homestead are the single most important source for peasant households in Wollo, as in many parts of the Ethiopian highlands. Natural woodland is nearly exhausted in Wollo and is not as reliable a source as in other regions of Ethiopia. Similar findings are reported by another study, which found that only 13% of the peasant associations in Wollo rely on natural forests as a source of fuelwood.[38] The contribution of community forests to peasant wood supply is insignificant, even when the trees are ready for harvest, due to the absence of guidelines on the utilization of these trees. The main obstacles to attaining a substantial increase in the wood supply of peasant households are social, economic, and political (see Table 2.8).

Mainly for the purpose of clarification, two categories can be extracted from Table 2.8 with regard to why farmers did not plant trees. In the first category belong 40% of the respondents, who blamed nature: 29% indicated that their seedlings did not survivie; 11% reported that there were enough indigenous bushes in their community. The second category represents the remaining 60%, whose reasons were socioeconomic and political: fear of confiscation and resettlement, a shortage of land around the homestead, and lack of seedlings.

A closer examination of the farmers in the first category, particularly those who found their environment unsuitable for tree planting, shows two distinct groups of farmers living in different zones. The first was concentrated in the lowlands of Bati, Kobo, Habru, and Werebabo weredas. These districts, noted for their unreliable rainfall pattern, are a frequent site of drought and famine in Wollo. A number of these farmers attempted to plant trees, but abandoned planting due to extremely low chances of seedling survival. An example from this group was a fifty-five-year-old farmer who lived in a lowland and semiarid zone (Heto peasant association, 014, with relatively poor, sandy soil), 10

Table 2.8 Peasants' Major Reasons for Not Planting Trees

Reasons For Not Planting Trees	Number of Respondents	Percentage of Respondents
Trees do not survive well in their environment	43	29
Shortage of land around their homestead (tree planting competes with cropland)	33	22
Peasant association will take trees outside their homestead	27	18
Enough natural bushes to use for fuel in the community	16	11
Seedlings not available	12	8
Peasant Association had previously taken what they planted	10	7
Fear they will be resettled	7	5
Total	148	100

A mother and child collect wood—an arduous task in the highlands of Wollo, Tebasit, Dessie Zurie.

Dung, a major source of fuel, is sold at the market, Haike, Ambassel.

kilometers away from the town of Bati. This farmer had planted eucalyptus seedlings, but they did not last through the long dry season. The only trees with any chance of survival, he added, were the indigenous bushes and acacia from which farmers cut the branches and replant. Like most of the farmers in the Bati area, this farmer did not face a shortage of fuelwood, because he used indigenous bushes and acacia from the vast lowlands.

The second group of farmers was made up mainly of those from the Alpine zones (elevation over 3,200 meters). A considerable number of these farmers lived in Dessie Zurie Awraja (Guguftu and Tebasit peasant associations) and Werehiminu Awraja (Akesta peasant association). In these peasant associations, as in the five neighboring ones at altitudes between 3,000 and 3,500 meters, there was no trace of trees. Almost 100% of the fuel supply in these peasant associations came from dung. These were monocropping areas where only barley was cultivated once a year because of the extended growing period due to the severe cold. The only vegetation here was a grassy shrub known as *cherfe*, which farmers used along with dung for fuel and as a material for roof cover.

An example from this group was a fifty-two-year-old farmer from Dessie Zurie Wereda (Guguftu peasant association), whose house was located 3,350 meters above sea level near the Wele mountains. This farmer spent over three years building his house, because he had to buy and transport the wood from the nearest town, Wereilu Awraja, 40 kilometers away. For him, as well as for the executive members of this peasant association, villagization (which refers to the government program of building new houses on newly selected sites or villages) would involve dismantling his present home and building a new one in a different location: a grim alternative he did not like to contemplate as it would take him another several years to build a new house. Most of the farmers in this peasant association also indicated that as children they had not seen any natural forest in this area; nor had they heard of any from their parents.

Of the respondents who gave socioeconomic reasons for not planting trees (60%), the largest groups were those who felt insecure about their rights to tree ownership in the peasant association and those who were insecure about government policies on resettlement. These insecurities are due to the lack of clear laws governing ownership and utilization of trees. Trees outside the immediate vicinity of the farm house (usually within 50 square meters) do not belong to the owner and can be confiscated by peasant associations. In fact, 7% of the farmers indicated that the trees they planted had been confiscated by the peasant associations. There were several cases where even trees within a farmer's compound could not be used without permission from the peasant association.

A tragic consequence of the absence of legal rights to trees and peasant associations' arbitrary decisions to confiscate them was seen in one of the most inaccessible peasant associations, Abaselama (012), of Kutaber Wereda, 15 kilometers from the town of Kutaber. This peasant association extends from 3,200 meters to approximately 2,000 meters above sea level and therefore includes *wurch*, highland, and medium altitude zones. To get to this scenic peasant association, one confronts the challenge of an uphill journey from the town of Kutaber, at 2,650 meters, to the peak of the hill (known as Negarit) at 3,250 meters above sea level. Finally, one must descend the rugged escarpment, which serves as a gateway to this peasant association.

The landmark of this peasant association is a gully (caused by severe downhill flooding), which begins at the top of the hill and extends for several kilometers along the road until reaches the plain. In 1976, shortly after the Agrarian Reform, the peasant association mobilized its members to plant trees in an attempt to arrest the expansion of the gully into the croplands. Few of the seedlings survived, because nobody assumed the responsibility of caring for them.

Realizing that individual initiatives were needed to ensure the survival of trees, the extension agent promised the farmers living near the gully entitlement to ownership of the trees that grew on this wasteland. In its twisted journey downward, the gully came within 20 meters of the house of one of the farmers interviewed for this study. The farmer took up the formidable task of planting eucalyptus seedlings in 1979, adding manure, building fences around the seedlings, and watering during the dry season. The fruits of his labor became evident as the seedlings stood taller than most of the huts around the area. His success became a subject of conversation in the village. Either out of envy or a plot organized by members or leaders of the peasant association, he was accused in July 1987 of planting trees on pathways belonging to the peasant association. The judiciary committee of the peasant association revoked his ownership of the trees, instructing him not to plant other seedlings around the gully.

The author of this study brought this farmer's case to the Head of the Ministry of Agriculture in Dessie Zurie Awraja. The following week the head of the Ministry of Agriculture for Dessie Zurie Awraja came to meet the farmer and the peasant association leaders. After the meeting, which involved a formal appeal and discussions, the decision to revoke the farmer's rights was reversed. However, there are limits to individual intervention. What is urgently needed in Ethiopia is an unambiguous policy to establish legal rights to individual owner- ship of trees. The exemplary efforts undertaken by this farmer were not made elsewhere because of insecurity about tree ownership.

Socioeconomic forces, particularly the lack of incentive to plant trees, have been identified as obstacles to increasing the wood supply in Wollo, according to a study done by the Red Cross, which runs a disaster prevention program that focuses on the rehabilitation of degraded lands in two catchments in Ambassel and Kalu awrajas.[39] The Swedish International Development Authority, which is involved in the rehabilitation of the Wollo region, has emphasized the importance of legal rights to tree ownership in the success of forestry projects.[40] Similarly, a recent study, which evaluated the United Nations World Food Program rehabilitation projects in the catchment areas in Hararghe, Gamo Gofa, North Shoa, and Wollo, pointed out that peasants, peasant association leaders, and even technicians were not certain who owned the trees planted in the project areas. [41] Thus, any government policy dealing with the rehabilitation of degraded land or afforestation would be futile unless it defined the individual farmer's role in this effort, and provided him with some security for utilizing his produce.

Utilization is closely related to issues of tree ownership. During the fieldwork, both agents for the Ministry of Agriculture and the Workers Party of Ethiopia (the party in power) delivered extensive sermons on the protection and the importance of trees, issues of which most peasants were fully aware. Yet, there was no discussion about utilization of trees by peasants and their communities. Indeed, irrespective of the projects under which trees had been planted, not a single farmer we interviewed mentioned receiving any benefits from the trees he planted. Trees do not have ornamental value for peasant households. Afforestation projects should include plans on how and when peasants will acquire benefits, and peasants should be informed of these benefits. Such planning and information is clearly absent in afforestation programs at present.

Another major policy issue that discouraged the planting of trees was the threat of resettlement (as reported by 5% of the respondents). The farmers who feared resettlement were in fact from peasant associations where many people left for resettlement during the 1984/85 famine, places which were also a focus of the resettlement program during this study. In Wollo, resettlement was a more serious threat than villagization. (The effects of resettlement on protection of natural resource will be explained in detail below.)

Among those respondents classified in the socioeconomic category were a large number (22%) who cited shortage of land, particularly around their homestead, as a reason for not planting trees. An examination of these respondents revealed the following:

1. The size of the cultivated land belonging to 60% of the respondents was under one hectare. Those whose holdings were between 1 and 1.5 hectares account for 31% of the respondents, and those whose holdings were between 1.5 and 2 hectares made up 9%. Thus, there was a significant statistical relationship between the amount of one's cultivated land and one's motivation to plant trees.
2. The majority of these farmers live in medium altitude zones (61%), 27% lived in highland zones, and a few (12%) lived in the lowland zones. Because farmers in the highland and medium altitudes faced a serious shortage of cultivable land (as discussed previously), and because the land around their homesteads was used for cultivation, tree planting competed with cropping.
3. Most of the respondents lived in smaller peasant associations where the availability of cropped land was shrinking due to land degradation and relatively large membership. A number of these respondents were from the Ashinga peasant association in Sayent Wereda (Borena Awraja),

with a peasant association size of 800 hectares and 781 heads of households. Others were from the Ambamariam in Mekedela Wereda (Werehiminu Awraja), with 800 hectares and 814 heads of households. Still others were from the Gala Giorgis in Gubalafto Wereda (Yeju Awraja), with 450 hectares and 458 heads of households. Finally, another group was from the Hara peasant association in Ambassel Wereda, with 800 hectares and 970 heads of households.

With due respect to limitation of land for planting trees in some communities, an in-depth discussion with a few of the farmers after the interview revealed that shortage of land could not always be taken as a reliable response. It is likely that insecurity of tree ownership may have greatly influenced decisions not to plant trees. To be sure, farmers have a chronic shortage of cropland in the peasant associations listed above. But there are numerous gullies and degraded lands in all these peasant associations, land which belongs to no one, and on which farmers could plant trees. Farmers could also benefit from planting trees around their homesteads as fences. For example, a thirty-five-year-old farmer (with three children under the age of six) in the Ambamariam peasant association owned three-quarters of a hectare of which he cultivated half a hectare. He lived on the upper slope where there were severely degraded lands and gullies close to his homestead. Every year he planted trees in the nearby state forest on the hill (called Jeru Amba) through the Food for Work Program. His major complaint was not that he had not seen any benefits from the trees he planted (which he thought belonged to the government anyway), but that he had not received food ration from the Food for Work Program for nearly a year for his labor contribution, as promised by the extension agents.

After the interview, the author informally asked the farmer why other farmers like himself were not planting trees in the expanding gullies that do not belong to anyone. The farmer humorously pointed out that there was a possibility of getting food through the Food for Work Program when he planted on the state farm, but that there would be little benefit from planting on the wasteland. However, this farmer seemed convinced that the issue was not so much whether the land was wasteland but whether planting on land that was not his would be looking for trouble from the peasant association. It is interesting to note that when peasants were pressed for reasons why they did not make use of degraded land around their homesteads and villages (an issue that puts them on the defensive), they expressed themselves in sophisticated Amharic nuances, saying that they were not certain of their rights to the trees they planted on their homestead, much less to trees growing on land that belonged to the peasant association.

Among the respondents who gave socioeconomic reasons for not planting trees are those who indicated the unavailability of seedlings (8%). This problem was due partly to a lack of nurseries and partly to a lack of infrastructure to transport the seedlings. In fact, most of the respondents who reported the unavailability of seedlings lived in peasant associations in Wadela Delanta Awraja (Delanta Wereda). The roads from Dessie to Wadela Delanta are some of the most difficult in Wollo and are inaccessible by four-wheel vehicles during the rainy season. Wadela Delanta is among the most severely degraded awrajas in Wollo, and yet there are few nurseries there and considerably fewer extension agents than in other awrajas, partly because of the remoteness of the area and partly due to the government policy of committing relatively few resources to awrajas with limited development potential. A number of farmers who lived in Werebabo Wereda (Ambassel Awraja) also cited the unavailability of seedlings as a reason for not planting trees. This wereda is also inaccessible by car during the rainy season when most planting activities take place.

The absence of clear policy guidelines regarding ownership and utilization of trees is the most severe impediment peasant farmers face in planting trees on their homesteads, in gullies and on wastelands. Reducing population growth, a measure that could decrease the demand for wood, would take at least a generation even with effective government policy. Hence, a national policy that encourages private initiative in planting trees is the most viable option in the effort to increase the country's wood supply as well in arresting deforestation in the immediate future.

Notes

1. *Ethiopia: Recent Economic Developments and Prospects for Recovery and Growth*, Washington, D.C.: The World Bank, 1987, p. 13.

2. Kenneth Newcombe, *An Economic Justification for Rural Afforestation: The Case of Ethiopia*, Washington, D.C.: The World Bank, 1984.

3. M. Constable and Members of the Ethiopian Highland Reclamation Study, *The Degradation of Resources and an Evaluation of Actions to Combat It*, Working Paper 19, Ministry of Agriculture, Addis Ababa, December 1984, pp. 1- 6.

4. W. H. Wishmeier, and D. D. Smith, *Predicting Rainfall Erosion Losses—A Guide to Conservation Planning*, Agricultural Handbook No. 537, Washington D.C.: United States Department of Agriculture, 1978.

5. Hans Humi, *Soil Conservation in Ethiopia, Guidelines for Development Agents in Ethiopia*, Ministry of Agriculture, Addis Ababa, Ethiopia, 1986. See also: M. Constable and Members of the Ethiopian Highlands Reclamation Team, *Annexes*, Ministry of Agriculture, Addis Ababa, May 1985, Annex 6, p. 3.

6. Hans Humi, *Erosion, Productivity, Conservation Systems in Ethiopia*, Paper Presented at the IV International Conference on Soil Conservation, Maracay, Venezuela, November 1985, p. 11.

7. Hans Humi, "Degradation and Conservation of Resources in the Ethiopian

Highlands," *Mountain Research and Development*, Vol. 8, Nos. 2/3, 1988, pp. 123-130.

8. Hans Hurni, *Applied Soil Conservation Research in Ethiopia*, Third National Workshop on Soil Conservation in Kenya, Department of Agricultural Engineering, Nairobi University, September 1986, p. 10.

9. Central Statistical Authority, *Area by Region, Awraja, Wereda in Square Kilometer, Gasha, Hectare*, Statistical Bulletin 49, February 1986, p. 30.

10. Ministry of Agriculture, *Ethiopia: Livestock Sector Review, Main Report*, prepared by Australian Agricultural Consulting and Management Company Ltd., Addis Ababa, p. 12.

11. K. N. N. S. Nair, *Ethiopia: Economic Analysis of Land Use*, Rome: Food and Agricultural Organization of the United Nations, 1986, p. 35.

12. Ministry of Agriculture, *Feeds and Forage Projects*, Project Preparation Report, Prepared by Australian Agricultural Consulting and Management Company Ltd., Addis Ababa, March 1985, pp. 8-9.

13. Nair, *Ethiopia*, p. 35.

14. Ministry of Agriculture, *Feeds and Forage Projects*, pp. 8-9.

15. Nair, *Ethiopia*, pp. 72-74.

16. Constable et al., *Annexes*, Annex 6, p. 10.

17. Garret Hardin, "The Tragedy of the Commons," *Science*, 163, 1968, pp. 1243-1248.

18. Gill Shepherd, *The Reality of the Commons: Answering Hardin from Somalia*, London: Overseas Development Institute, Social Forestry Network, Network Paper 6d, 1988.

19. E. Westphal, *Plus in Ethiopia, their taxonomy and agricultural significance*, Joint publication by College of Agriculture, Haile Sellassie University and the Agricultural University, Wageningen, the Netherlands, Wageningen, February 1974.

20. Yersawork Admassie, Mulugate Abebe, Markos Ezara, and J. Gay, *Report on the Sociological Survey and Sociological Considerations in Preparing a Development Strategy*, Ethiopian Highland Reclamation Study, Ministry of Agriculture, Addis Ababa, 1983, p. 51-54.

21. Constable et al., *Degradation of Resources*, p. 23.

22. Hans Hurni, *Ecological Issues in the Creation of Famines in Ethiopia*, Paper presented on a Disaster Prevention and Preparedness Strategy for Ethiopia, December 5-8, 1988, Addis Ababa, pp. 9-10.

23. M. Constable and members of the Ethiopian Highland Reclamation Study, *Development Strategy*, Working Paper 24, Ministry of Agriculture, Addis Ababa, May 1985, p. 41.

24. Central Statistical Authority, *Population Situation in Ethiopia—Past, Present, and Future*, Population Studies Series No. 1, Addis Ababa, March 1988, pp. 20-26. See also: Central Statistical Authority, *Population Projection of Ethiopia: Total and Sectoral (1985-2035)*, Population Studies Series No. 2, Addis Ababa, March 1988, p. 30.

25. Central Statistical Authority, *Population Situation in Ethiopia*, p. 11.

26. Central Statistical Authority, *Population Projection of Ethiopia*, p. 20.

27. International Union for Conservation of Nature and Natural Resources, *Ethiopia: Land-Use Planning and Natural Resource Conservation*, Gland, Switzerland, 1986, p. 53.

28. Ministry of Agriculture, *General Agricultural Survey*, Addis Ababa, 1984.

29. Dessalegn Rahmato, *Famine and Survival Strategies: A Case Study from Northeast Ethiopia*, Institute of Development Research, Addis Ababa, May 1987, p. 51.

30. Alemneh Dejene, *Peasants, Agrarian Socialism, and Rural Development in Ethiopia*, Boulder, Colo.: Westview Press, 1987, pp. 56-57.

31. Ester Boserup, *Population and Technological Change: A Study of Long-Term Trends*, Chicago: The University of Chicago Press, 1983.

32. Mark R. Mujwahuzi, "The Impact of Population Growth on Food Production in Tanzania: Problems and Prospects," in Fassil G. Kiros, *Challenging Rural Poverty: Experience in Institution Building and Popular Participation for Rural Development in East Africa*, Trenton, N.J.: African World Press, 1985.

33. Lester Brown, *State of the World*, A World Watch Institute Report on Progress Toward a Sustainable Society, New York: Norton, 1985, pp. 11-12. See also: Eneas Salati and Peter B. Vose, "Amazon Basin: A System in Equilibrium," *Science*, July 13, 1984.

34. Brown, *State of the World*, p. 12.

35. The World Bank, *Ethiopia: Forestry Project*, Washington D.C., May 1986, p. 2.

36. Data generated from the Ministry of Agriculture Zonal Office in Dessie, Wollo, February 1988.

37. The World Bank, *Ethiopia: Forestry Project*, p. 3.

38. Ezra, Markos and Kassahun Berhanu, *A Review of the Community Forestry Programme and an Evaluation of its Achievements: A Socio-Economic Survey*, Addis Ababa, 1988, p. 50.

39. Marten Bendz and Per A. Molin, *Trees Grow in Wollo*, Ethiopian Red Cross Society, Upper Mille & Cheleka Catchments Disaster Prevention Program, 1987.

40. SIDA Support to Wollo Region, Background Papers, SIDA Wollo Mission, September to December, Addis Ababa, 1986. Two pertinent articles on the issues of legal rights to trees are presented in this background paper: Martin Adams, "Community Forestry in Ethiopia: Some Preliminary Thoughts," Working Paper No. 1., p. 8.; Jan Hultin "The Predicament of Peasants in Conservation Based Development," Working Paper No. 8, p. 2-3.

41. Yeraswork Admassie, *Impact and Sustainability of Activities for Rehabilitation of Forest, Grazing and Agricultural Lands*, United Nations World Food Program, Addis Ababa, September 1988, pp. 38-42.

3

Environmental Threat: Peasants'
Perceptions and Actions

A widely misunderstood subject in Ethiopia is the peasants' perceptions of their environment. It is misunderstood partly because outsiders, both "experts" and policymakers, who write about peasants and formulate policies, often have limited understanding about the peasants' environment. This lack of access to representation contributes to what Paul Richards calls "the desystemization of peasant knowledge and practice" about the indigenous ecology of Africa.[1] Furthermore, a peasant's view of the environment is often ignored without due consideration to the predicament he faces between survival and environmental exploitation. The vicious circle of survival and environmental degradation, as articulated in the works of Piers Blaikie, Micheal Watts, Brian Spooner, and H.S. Mann is vital in an understanding of peasants' actions and in our own attempt to prevent environmental degradation.[2]

The environmental threats to Ethiopian agriculture are an extensively debated issue. Numerous cursory consultancy reports have been written and policy recommendations made on the subject. The Ethiopian government and donor agencies have formulated one policy after another to combat ecological degradation, often on an impressionistic basis about the nature and the magnitude of the problem. There are few village-level data that identify the socioeconomic forces that fuel the process of environmental degradation. After all, as Micheal Watts put it, "desertification and environmental degradation is an ultimately local, place-specific process and must be understood as such."[3]

Environmental degradation in Ethiopia is synonymous with land degradation. In an attempt to identify the process of land degradation at the village level, some of the indicators developed by Priscilla Reining[4] and Harold Dregne[5] to monitor desertification were selectively used. These indicators include some of the major indicators such as soil erosion, soil fertility, soil depth, the level of stoniness, rainfall variability, and water and fuelwood availability. This study, however, puts major emphasis on soil erosion since it is the primary source of degradation in the Ethiopian highlands and deeply affects the quality of the rooting conditions. One of the measurements of land quality identified by the Ministry of Agriculture Land Use Planning Department is the soil rooting conditions, which are influenced by soil depth and the level of stoniness. Hence, soil erosion is the most pertinent indicator in an attempt to understand the process of degradation at the household level in Ethiopia.

Soil Erosion

Soil erosion is difficult to measure even when the means and the resources are available. The dilemma in measuring soil erosion in developing countries is well documented by Piers Blaikie, who said that lack of resources, sophisticated equipment, and trained manpower and the need for a longitudinal measurement make it difficult to measure soil loss.[6] Needless to say, measuring soil loss was not possible for a one-man study with limited resources, nor was such a measurement relevant to the objective of this study. The level of erosion, whether it is "very severe," "severe," or "minor," is determined by peasant experience and perceptions and is therefore a relative term. The underlying issue in posing these questions is to ascertain the farmers' awareness of soil erosion.

During the interview, the peasants' views on the level of erosion were first elicited and subsequently verified by on-the-spot observation of the farming plot under consideration by the team of experienced extension agents working with the author. As pointed out above, farmers were generally guarded in expressing their views about environmental degradation. This was because one of the criteria for resettlement, which was viewed as an enormous threat to the peasantry in Wollo, was the level of degradation. It was, therefore, logical for farmers to conceal information that might make them targets for resettlement.

With due respect for this limitation, farmers were asked about the level of erosion on their main cropland. This does not mean that the soil erosion on grazing land, unproductive land, or other minor plots a farmer cultivates is not as significant. Rather, the focus is on assessing the level of erosion on cropland because there is still no empirical data to refute Hans Hurni's findings that soil loss in Ethiopia is highest on cropland. Moreover, it was easier for farmers to remember the conditions on the cropland and for us to verify them; and other related indicators of degradation, such as soil depth and the level of stoniness, are more easily observed on cropland. With this limitation in the background, peasant views on the level of erosion are presented in Table 3.1, which presents two somewhat contradictory results because of the strong incentive not to tell the truth. On the one hand, the majority of the farmers (68%) seemed to be frank in expressing the incidence of erosion. On the other hand, they seemed to be restrained and calculating in expressing how seriously they were affected by the level of erosion. Consequently, those who indicated facing a severe problem of erosion were in the minority (26%), whereas those having a minor problem (42%) and no problem (31%) were in the majority. There has been no other survey undertaken in Wollo with which to compare these findings. However,

Table 3.1 Peasants' Perceptions of Level of Erosion on the Main Plot

Level of Erosion	Number of Respondents	Percentage of Respondents
Very Severe	3	1
Severe	58	25
Minor	96	42
No Problem	71	31
Not Certain	2	1
Total	230	100

one of the few sociological surveys, taken in 1980, covering ten of the administrative regions (including Wollo), indicated that 69% of the farmers reported experiencing a high level of erosion on their plots.[7]

On the whole, the findings in Table 3.1 suggest that the farmers' responses are reliable only to a certain extent. Field investigation of the main plot after the interview revealed a discrepancy between what the farmers reported and what was actually observed. In view of the difference between the reported and observed levels of erosion, two patterns emerged. In the first case, farmers in the same peasant association, affected by a more or less similar magnitude of erosion, gave responses that contradicted one another. In the second case, most of the respondents in the peasant association uniformly underrated the seriousness of the problem, mainly because of the threat of resettlement.

An example of the first case, in which a farmer's response was in sharp contrast with other farmers' responses in the same peasant association, occurred in Legambo Wereda (Werehiminu Awraja), in a hilly peasant association (Akesta, 01) severely affected by famine. This particular farmer's house was located close to the top of the hill at 3,020 meters above sea level. His major plot, 0.5 hectare, was located on the upper slope at 2,900 meters. This forty-eight-year-old farmer reported that he had no problem of erosion when, in fact, nearly all the dark clay topsoil usually found at such high elevation was eroded and had been replaced by thin, sandy soil. The level of erosion on this plot, without a doubt, was very severe. This farmer also consistently underrated the other indicators of degradation. The most obvious one, the quantity of stones on the main plot, he reported to be minor, when it was actually severe. A large number of stones suggests a substantial decrease in soil depth. On the other hand, other respondents in this peasant association whose major plots were on the upper and lower slope reported having severe problems. The accounts of these farmers were close to our observation.

There were some exceptions in which a farmer's claim of having no problem of erosion in a highly degraded peasant association were in fact true.

An example was a twenty-four-year-old farmer who lived in a highland zone, Dewate peasant association (02) of Sayent Wereda (Borena Awraja), highly affected by erosion. This peasant association extends from the town of Ajibar, located on a plateau at a medium altitude of 2,780 meters, to a lowland zone close to a gorge of the Nile River, bordering the Gojam region. The Chilaga River, one of the tributaries of the Nile, paves its way by amassing soil debris from the hills and valleys of this peasant association.

This farmer had four plots, of which the main and the most fertile was located on the lower slope below 2,000 meters above sea level; the rest of his plot and his house were located on the upper slope at 2,700 meters above sea level. He pointed out that while his least fertile plot was on the upper slope and was highly affected by erosion, he seldom faced this problem on his major plot, located in the valley because topsoil carried from the upper slope was deposited on his plot. This farmer's response illustrates what is known as the "downstream effect," the deposition of sediments from runoff and floods from the highlands and upper slopes onto the lower altitude areas and valleys. Sediments have high nutrient content and in the short-term could increase land productivity. But their overall impact, as explained in the Highland Reclamation Study, is negative.[8]

To be sure, it is the downstream effect that enriches Egypt, but the amount of topsoil carried down in Wollo is not enough for sustained cropping and is quickly covered by less fertile subsoil sediments. A classic example of this was witnessed in Kobo Wereda where the farming system depends on diverting floods from the nearby highland areas of Lasta Awraja. Most cultivation in the valley of Kobo Wereda takes place during the long rainy season (*meher*), mainly because of the region's reliance on floods. During the *meher* season, the farmers engineer the direction of the "downstream effect" from the highland areas, which are 20 to 30 kilometers away from their farms. Asked if this practice was beneficial, one of the interviewed farmers responded: "Of course! there are farmers who have lost their lives to bring the floods to their farms."

However, a closer examination of the farms that rely on flooded water and the deposition of sediments and those that do not reveals that this practice is likely to lead to the decline of soil fertility in the long run. For instance, the Gala Mangelo peasant association (016), about 15 kilometers south of Kobo, does not use extensive flooding and has light brown soil, whereas the Neguisgale peasant association (03), about 20 kilometers north of the town of Kobo, depends heavily on diverting floods and has very thin, sand-like soil. During the dry season, the dominant topsoil structure in the Neguisgale peasant association (like most parts of Kobo that depend on floods) is composed of shiny sand-like sediments that have been deposited during the rainy season. This soil does not have much nutrient content to build the soil structure and improve rooting conditions. It is very light and easily eroded by wind (another indicator of desertification), which is very severe during the dry season in this area. The sediments also prevent drainage, limiting the availability of oxygen around the

Table 3.2 Farmers' Perceptions of the Level of Soil Erosion in Peasant
Associations that Are Given High Priority for Resettlement

Location of Peasant Association	Level of Severity of Erosion					Number of Respondents
	Very Severe	Severe	Minor	No Problem	Not Certain	
Borena Awraja						
Ashinga PA (01)	—	1	1	3	—	5
Werehiminu Awraja						
Chacha PA (08)	—	—	4	1	—	5
Wadela Delanta						
Goshmeda PA (032)	—	—	3	2	—	5
Ambassel Awraja						
Gishen PA (034)	—	1	4	—	—	5
Yeju Awraja						
Gala Giorgis PA (013)	—	1	2	2	—	5

root zone. This experience in Kobo suggests that one indicator of environmental degradation (desertification) is inextricably linked to another. In the case of Kobo, the downstream effect contributes to wind erosion, poor soil drainage, reduced soil depth and fertility, all of which are indicators of degradation.

The respondents who had to some extent uniformly underrated the level of erosion lived in highly eroded peasant associations that were given high priority under the resettlement program. In these peasant associations, there had been an active campaign by party officials and extension agents to recruit families for resettlement. These peasant associations and the peasants' views towards the level of erosion are presented in Table 3.2.

In spite of some variation in their topographies, all the peasant associations presented in Table 3.2 had numerous gullies, spectacular gorges, and steep escarpments. Yet, most of the farmers interviewed reported having either no problems of erosion or minor levels of erosion. These peasants' views differed substantially from the findings obtained through field verification, with the exception of the few farmers whose major plots were located in the valley. It is difficult to imagine that any piece of land would remain untouched by erosion in these areas. In some of them, the downstream effect, in the absence of soil to transport, had lead to stone erosion. This means that as the amount of soil diminishes, heavy flooding increasingly carries stones from the top of the hill and upper slopes and deposits them at the bottom of the hill. Such stone accumulation at the base of the hill had made oxen ploughing a strenuous task.

All the peasant associations cited above had high priority in the government resettlement program. They were also among the peasant associations identified as seriously affected by the 1987 drought and in need of immediate relief assistance. A large number of families were also resettled from these peasant associations during the 1984 famine.

The Ethiopian government's assertion that most of the land in these peasant associations was unsuitable for agriculture, highly degraded, and should be under area closure to regenerate appears to have been valid. Under these circumstances, resettlement, if implemented properly, was also a legitimate option in dealing with the problem of environmental degradation. Yet, the fear of resettlement became a major obstacle to undertaking conservation activities that could minimize the level of degradation (this dilemma will be explored in detail below).

During the fieldwork, it became evident that soil erosion, seen largely as a highland problem, was a problem of equal magnitude in the medium altitude zones and in some of the lowland zones. In this survey, the number of respondents indicating the incidence of erosion on their main plots (taking into account the difference in the level of severity) was 75% in the highland, 72% in the medium altitude, and 60% in the lowland zone. The peasant associations that were most affected by erosion in the lowland zones were exclusively in Werebabo and Bati weredas, where, instead of the characteristic flatness of the lowland areas, chains of small hills are a common sight. Particularly in Bati, rows of small hills with corresponding tiny valleys separating one from the other extend in every direction. Barren hills of worn-out sandy soils and considerable stones are everywhere in the lowlands of Bati and Werebabo and in the highlands of Sayent, Delanta, and Ambassel weredas.

In sharp contrast to what was observed in the highlands, peasants in Bati and Werebabo weredas were more candid in expressing their observations of indicators of ecological degradation. In most cases, the peasants' reports were similar to our own observations. These areas were not well suited to cultivation and most of the inhabitants seemed to be more interested in livestock than in crop farming. The majority of the population in Bati and Werebabo are ethnically Oromos and distant relatives of nomadic tribes that roam the lowlands.

Farmers were asked if they had experienced a decline in soil depth and soil fertility and to what extent their plots were stony. These indicators augment and validate the farmers' previous responses to the issues of erosion, as they are also indirect measures of the level of erosion. Farmers were cautious in responding to these indicators, again for the same reason: fear of resettlement. Most farmers, however, found it difficult to respond to whether or not there had been a decline in soil depth. As a result, this concept was simplified by asking if they had observed a decrease in the amount of topsoil covering the plough since they started farming. In spite of this simplification, a large number of respondents, 31%, were "uncertain" about a decline in soil depth, whereas only 1% had given that response in regard to soil erosion. A considerable number, 41%, said they had observed a decrease, while 28% said they had not seen any decrease in topsoil. Of those who reported a decrease in soil depth, 54% had reported severe erosion, 39% minor erosion, and 6% no problem. Thus, a significant statistical relationship between the level of erosion and a decrease in soil depth was observed.

Another question that farmers had difficulty answering was whether they had observed a decrease in soil fertility on their main plots in normal years. In an attempt to simplify it, the question was phrased, "Have you seen a decrease in yield, in times of adequate rainfall, since you started farming on the major plot?" Forty-two percent indicated that they had not seen a decrease in soil fertility, 30% had seen a minor decrease, 17% had seen a severe decrease, and 11% said they were not certain. Nearly all of the respondents who reported a decrease in soil fertility were affected by soil erosion, indicating a significant statistical relationship between the two variables.

There was also a statistical relationship between the level of erosion and the extent of stoniness on the main plot, as 60% of those who reported having a great deal of stones on the major plot were also affected by erosion. (The presence of a large number of stones is usually the result of severe soil erosion, except in the few cases when stones are transported along with soil from the top of the hill or mountain to the bottom of the slope). Soil fertility, however, did not always correspond to the extent of stoniness. Some farmers pointed out that their relatively fertile plot had a considerable amount of stones. Most of these farmers lived in highland peasant associations. A good example was a forty-five-year-old farmer in Wereilu Wereda, Adama peasant association (019). His largest and most fertile plot (0.75 hectare), located at an elevation of 3,100 meters, was severely affected by erosion and very stony. Yet, he considered this plot to be relatively fertile because the stones protected the seeds from wind and water erosion during the germination period.

This was a rational response, because the growing period at such an elevation is longer and the likelihood that seeds can easily be swept away by erosion is greater. Some peasants in both the highland and lowland areas also pointed out that stones helped maintain moisture content during the dry season. Discussion with local extension agents and field observation suggested that stones (unless they were in great magnitude) were unlikely to be a major obstacle in peasant farming which uses a single plough driven by oxen. Hence, the level of stoniness, which may be an important indicator of desertification in other regions where it could interfere with ploughing and seed bed preparation, particularly in mechanized farming, is not a good indicator of soil degradation and fertility in Ethiopia.

Rainfall Variability

Shortage of rainfall, given by farmers as the primary reason for crop failure, was also cited in numerous reports that circulated in the Ministry of Agriculture and the Relief and Rehabilitation Commission. Most of the peasants in lowland areas were more severely affected by the 1984/85 famine and the 1987 drought than those in the highland and medium altitudes. In examining the rainfall data of both the communities that were severely affected by recurrent famine and those communities where the impact was limited, a great variance in the amount of rainfall these communities received was observed. One of the few communities where a considerable number of interviewed farmers indicated not being affected by the 1984 famine and having enough "food reserve" to last them until the next harvest lived in Rike (Dinkye Gobensa and Dinkye Gelana peasant associations), Eseyegola Wereda. (These two peasant associations in Rike are

Table 3.3 Amount of Rainfall in Rike, Eseyegola Wereda (millimeters)

Years						Months							
	Jan	Feb	Mar	Apr	May	Jun	Jul	Aug	Sep	Oct	Nov	Dec	Total
68	0	106	18	142.4	8	84.8	411.9	195.4	68.2	5	69.5	3	1,112.2
69	96.1	159.9	144.5	131.1	68.5	11	250.8	225.7	49	31	0	0	1,167.6
70	51.0	55	106	84	5	0	276	329	103	20	0	8	1,737.0
71	7	0	51	56	149	5	216	256	85.2	3.7	94.5	70.2	993.6
72	0	89.1	76.4	122	46.9	113.8	247.6	121.2	57.4	30	0	0	904.4
73													—
74	0	10.9	116.8	31.6	68.8	99.5	224.3	362.1	198.1	4.9	0	0	1,117.0
75	52	55.1	16.5	42.8	40.9	81.6	256.8	348.5	144	0	0	43	1,081.2
76	0	50.8	51.8	177.5	62.9	53	416.3	366.6	117.3	62	79.8	9.9	1,447.9
77	119.7	12	5	123	100.6	3	479.9	355.2	106	190.2	0	0	1,494.6
78	0	46.9	37.9	28.6	34.6	28.9	243.8	207.3	94.1	18.5	18	66.9	825.5
79	91.3	15.7	53	10.9	157.4	59.4	160.2	274.4	163.2	124.7	0	22	1,132.2
80	40.9	63.3	92	112	31.5	0	282.1	280.3	102.2	72.1	29.2	0	1,105.6
81	0	0	333.3	115.5	0	0	385.1	516	181.5	88.2	0	38.1	1,657.7
82	135.6	8.2	30.9	157.8	144.3	0	224.6	161.7	197.2	367.3	226.9	85.8	1,740.3
83	22.2	43	120.1	116.4	111.6	30.1	151.1	202.4	30.6	43	0	0	870.5
84	4.1	8.3	52.7	14.3	184.7	17.4	109.7	24.8	110.9	0	0	58.5	585.4
85	9.6	0	46.6	325.1	82.4	0	207.1	314	148.2	17.2	0	17.3	1,167.5
86	0	53.5	41.8	107.7	29.9	189.1	198.4	369.6	203	5.8	0	79.3	1,278.1
87	0	63.6	250.4	188.5	329.8	2	16.9	284.8	66	52.2	0	104.6	1,358.8
88	15	85.6	0	183.7	0	29.8	412.3	354.4	295.8	67	0	0	1,443.6

Total													23,520.7
Average													1,176.0

Source: National Meteorological Services Agency, Addis Ababa
Note: No data available for 1973.

those that practice the agroforestry to be discussed below.) On the other hand, Bati was devastated by the 1984 famine and severely affected by the 1987 drought. The amount of rainfall from 1968 to 1988 in Rike and Bati is presented in Tables 3.3 and 3.4 respectively.

In comparing the rainfall data in Tables 3.3 and 3.4 we find the following:

1. The average annual rainfall from 1968 to 1988 (excluding 1973 for Rike for which there were no data), was 1,176.03 millimeters for Rike and 829.6 millimeters for Bati.
2. The least amount of average annual rainfall recorded in both Rike and Bati was in 1984: 585.4 millimeters for Rike and 310.6 millimeters for Bati. Bati also had the third lowest rainfall in twenty years (641.8 millimeters) in 1973, which was another major famine year experienced by many of the farmers interviewed in Bati. The lowest amount of rainfall in the last 20 years was also recorded in many weredas of Wollo that experienced the 1984 famine. For example, among the areas covered in this study, the average annual rainfall in Woldeyia (Yeju Awraja) was 543.9 millimeters; in Kombolcha (Kalu Awraja), 561.3 millimeters; in Kutaber (Dessie Zurie Awraja), 480.7 millimeters; and in Kobo (Raya & Kobo Awraja), 105.4 millimeters.[9] These figures give further evidence to support the peasants' assertion that rainfall was the single most important factor in crop failure, given the impact of the 1984 famine throughout Wollo.

Table 3.4 Amount of Rainfall in Bati, Bati Wereda (millimeters)

Years							Months						
	Jan	Feb	Mar	Apr	May	Jun	Jul	Aug	Sep	Oct	Nov	Dec	Total
68	0	96	36	157	0	21	269	86	64	0	53	30	812.0
69	73	232	15	108	44	0	267	69	47.9	14.9	0	0	870.8
70	111.9	42.8	108.9	23.2	50.7	1	292.3	194.7	140.9	6.5	0	6.5	979.4
71	46.3	2.3	11.5	40.2	142.2	6.6	136.2	192.3	43.5	26.2	112.2	108.3	867.8
72	0	21.6	50.9	113.3	35.9	167.2	136	108.4	168.3	5	0	17.6	824.2
73	15.2	0	0	16.5	110.7	0	157.7	220.1	87.4	13.6	0	20.6	641.8
74	0	6.3	149	11.5	68.9	108.6	196.5	169.8	139.2	0	0	0	849.8
75	0	0	7.4	92.3	70.7	34.9	191.9	282.6	129.7	5.4	0	21.4	836.3
76	37.3	5	33.2	90.4	120.1	25.3	100.1	269.1	24.5	28.4	27.5	5.8	766.7
77	39.8	5.6	0	17.6	17.3	5.2	196.8	279.4	88.3	114.2	169.4	0	933.6
78	19	79.7	35.8	154.9	15.8	0	160.7	252	108.1	33.6	5.5	79	944.1
79	195.9	78.2	85.3	106.1	14.4	1.4	79.1	286.2	27	38	0	23.9	935.5
80	13.2	44.1	49	36.5	13.9	0.8	186.3	174	68.5	15.8	4.1	0	606.2
81	0	0	164.9	86.2	22.3	0	159.9	260.9	21.1	0	0	9	724.3
82	94.4	0	0	92.1	25	0	66.3	150	72.6	111.7	170	76	858.1
83	68.1	62	121	174.2	194	1.2	147.6	160.5	51.9	49.1	0.5	1	1,031.1
84	6.8	7.7	9.1	13	112.1	18.2	18.6	33.2	50.8	0	0.6	40.5	310.6
85	17.8	0	19.9	155.4	24.2	8.9	188.1	236.2	75.4	2.6	0	20.6	749.1
86	0	132.5	80.4	85.5	73.4	89.7	220.1	326.8	82.8	3.8	0	47.8	1,142.8
87	1.7	28.1	112.5	129.0	170.9	2.5	49.1	228.3	46.1	48.2	0	36.3	852.7
88	0	32.4	5	71.5	10.4	19.6	357.2	225.9	129.9	19.5	0	13.4	884.8
Total													17,421.7
Average													829.6

Source: National Meteorological Services Agency, Addis Ababa

3. The amount of rainfall during the *belg* season (February, March and
April) was more below normal in 1984 in both Rike and Bati than in
other years, and it was also followed by another very low amount of
rainfall during the *meher* season (July, August, and September), particularly in Bati. Thus, the failure of rain in the *belg* season, unless
compensated for in the *meher* season, is a clear signal of widespread crop
failure and a famine year.

Altitude in Ethiopia influences the rainfall patterns. Most of the highland
areas have a rainfall above 1,400 millimeters and are considered wet zones,
whereas most of the lowlands are referred to as dry zones and receive below
900 millimeters of rainfall. The moist zone receives 900 to 1,400 millimeters of
rain and mostly includes medium altitude areas and some lowland and highland
areas.[10] As valid as this classification may be, the findings from Rike augments
the hypothesis that rainfall variability is more likely to be influenced by forest
cover. Rike, located between 2,000 and 2,150 meters above sea level, receives
more annual rainfall than many highland areas over 3,000 meters above sea
level. (For example, Rike has received an average rainfall of over 1,400
millimeters *five times* in the past nineteen years (see Table 3.3), whereas the
Dessie area, which extends from 2,600 to 3,000 meters above sea level, has
received rainfall of over 1,400 millimeters only once during the same one-year
period.[11]) Rike also has one of the most dense forest and vegetative covers of
the peasant association covered in this study, and this may have contributed to
the relatively higher amount and better distribution of rainfall.

Natural Forest: Myth or Reality?

An overwhelming number of farmers recognized the crucial role that trees and
forests play in their livelihood. A small number of respondents (2%) said they
had no opinion about trees, but these people lived in the lowland zones of Bati
and Werebabo, where they had enough natural bushes to meet their needs. The
most frequently cited uses of trees were for fuel, construction, farming equipment, shade for animals, and fences. The most popular tree species for both fuel
and construction in highland and medium altitude zones is *Eucalyptus globulus*,
followed by *Juniperus procera*. In the lowland zones, *Acacia abyssinica* is the
most widely used for both fuel and construction. Different species of acacia are
also frequently used in medium altitude zones. In the Alpine zones of over 3,200
meters above sea level, trees are scarce and the ground is covered by *Erica
arborea* (Amharic name *aseta*) and *cherfe* (its Amharic name), usually used for
fuel.

The highland of Wollo at one time was covered by *Juniperus procera*
(Amharic name *yebashea tid*) and *Olea africana* (Amharic name *weyera*). The

best testimonials to this are the church yards covered by these two species throughout Wollo. In areas where there were no traces of trees in the surroundings, *Juniperus procera* and *Olea africana* served as fences by completely surrounding Saint Michael Church at Tenta (Tenta Wereda, Werehiminu Awraja), Gishen Mariam Church at Gishen (Gishen Wereda, Ambassel Awraja), and Saint Gaberiel Church at Woldeyia (Gubalafto Wereda, Yeju Awraja). In addition, *Juniperus procera* regenerated quickly in the mountains and hills that were restricted recently, from both human and animal interference, by hillside closure. A good example are the hills on the road from Dessie to Ambassel where this species reappeared within a few years. This rapid regeneration confirms that the highlands are its natural habitat. The other common tree species that farmers indicated using for fuel and construction are *Corton macrostachys* (Amharic name *bisna*), *Dodonea viscosa* (*kitkita*), *Ficus vasta* (*woreka*), and *Zizyphus spina-christi* (*kurkura*).

Natural forests have for the most part disappeared in Wollo. Those that remain are scattered throughout Wollo and are estimated to total only 44,000 hectares, comprised mainly of shrubs and bushes with only a small amount covered by indigenous trees, such as *Juniperus procera*. The largest remaining natural forest is found in Borena Awraja at Denkoro (2,400 hectares). Why Denkoro natural forest has not diminished in size is an important question for further investigation. It would appear that its location and rugged topography may have contributed to its preservation. The Denkoro natural forest is in a gorge surrounded by mountains and covers an area that descends from a highland altitude of over 3,000 meters above sea level to a lowland zone that touches the gorges of the river Nile. The Denkoro area is virtually inaccessible by four-wheel drive and there are no towns near it.

The natural forest in Denkoro includes tree species that are not found anywhere in Wollo, at least not in any significant quantity (*Cordia abyssinica*, Amharic name *wanza*; *Podocarpus gracilior*, *zigba*; *Syzygium guineense*, *dokma*; and *Pygeum africanum*, *tikur inchet*). These trees, which are only found in the Denkoro natural forest in Wollo, are widespread in the western part of Ethiopia, particularly in the Keffa and Illubabor regions, where nearly all of Ethiopia's remaining natural forest is found.

Of the farmers included in this study, only 23% indicated having a natural forest in their community. What constituted a natural forest differed among and within communities. In some communities, the natural forest was bushes and shrubs (*chaka*), while in others it was woody vegetation and trees (*dene*). The kind of forest that farmers usually refer to as *dene* sometimes had pockets of *Juniperus procera* and *Olea africana*. Respondents in the same peasant association often gave conflicting views regarding the presence of a natural forest in their community. In several peasant associations, one or two indicated the presence of a natural forest in their community, whereas the rest said there was none. These discrepancies reflect the differing perceptions farmers had about what constitutes a natural forest. There were only two peasant associations (Dinkye Gobensa and Dinkye Gelana) in Eseyegola Wereda where all the respondents indicated that there was a natural forest. These very hilly peasant associations, where agroforestry was practiced, had reserved areas specifically for forest development. Of the 2,016 hectares of land in Dinkeye Gobensa (06), 1,402 were covered by forest, while Dinkeye Gelana (07) had 1,814 hectares of land of which 983 were covered by forest. These forests, mostly on the hills, were managed by and belonged to the Ministry of Agriculture State Forest Development Department.

The presence of a natural forest in a community did not indicate that there is no fuelwood shortage in the community. In fact, of those who reported having a natural forest in their community, dung was the major source of fuel for 40%, fuelwood for 36%, both dung and fuelwood for 19%, and crop residue for 4%. This confusion was again noticed in examining the incidence of soil erosion. A considerable number of farmers who indicated that there was a natural forest in their community were as affected by soil erosion as those farmers without a natural forest in their community. In addition, there was no statistical relationship between the incidence of erosion and the presence of a natural forest. Both of these findings confirm that what was considered a natural forest was likely to be merely a small quantity of bushes with a little vegetative cover.

Studies have pointed out that the clearing of forest cover due to the expansion of shifting cultivation is a major reason for the soil degradation and declining yields in Africa. Forests are an important source of vegetative biomass that enrich the soil with organic content and protect it from erosion.[12] The findings from these peasant associations in Rike, which have the highest proportion of area covered by forest among the peasant associations covered in this study, underscore the significance of forests and biomass cover. The smallest number of interviewed farmers experiencing the incidence of erosion and total crop failure in famine years were found here.

One of the indicators that is commonly used to assess the level of environmental degradation is the availability of fuelwood in a community. The total absence of fuelwood in many of the peasant associations included in this survey gives further evidence to the serious level of environmental degradation, particularly deforestation, in Wollo. In the lowland zones, crop residue, in the form of sorghum stalks, was the major source of fuel. In the sample, the largest group of farmers using crop residue lived in Kobo Wereda. In this predominantly lowland area, all of the farmers interviewed reported that crop residue constituted nearly the entire source of fuel. In addition, due to the extreme wood shortage, sorghum stalks were even used in the construction of huts.

Shortage of fuelwood was more widespread and severe in the *wurch* and highland zones, where over 95% of the respondents reported having a fuelwood shortage (followed by 79% in medium altitude zones, and 72% in lowland zones). These data are also supported by the fact that in the highland and *wurch* zones, dung constituted a large proportion of the entire fuel source. Hence, a significant statistical relationship was observed between the ecological zone in which a farmer lived and the shortage of fuelwood. The Ethiopian government effort in the restoration of forest cover for both fuel needs and conservation purposes concentrated on the promotion of community forest and area closure within peasant associations. However, these efforts face major problems and need careful examination in light of peasants' views and response to these activities.

Community Forest: An Ambiguous Existence

The approaches and the objectives of the community forest project differ widely from one country to another. To some, community forest means growing trees for environmental reasons, while to others, trees are to be used for meeting subsistence needs. Still others could use the community forest as a source of cash income.[13] The community forest was introduced in Ethiopia in 1980, primarily to meet the fuelwood and construction needs of the peasant and urban dwellers associations. The site for the community forest is selected by the peasant association leaders with the assistance of Ministry of Agriculture agents. In most cases the land allotted for the community forest (not more than five hectares) is not regarded as the best land.

The overwhelming number of farmers who indicated that they planted trees had done so in the community forest through a tree planting program organized by the peasant associations. Yet most farmers who planted trees in community forests saw them as part of the government-owned state forest. This suggests that no systematic information was provided by peasant association leaders or extension agents emphasizing that the community forests belonged to the association and its members. In addition, peasants were uninformed as to whether they would benefit from the trees they planted in the community forests. This uncertainty about who would be able to utilize forest products led to both the poor management of community forests as well as to the low survival rate of seedlings. Once again, the lack of clear legal rights regarding the ownership and the utilization of trees was an impediment to increasing fuelwood supply.

The degree of the farmers' unawareness of the existence of community forests in their own peasant associations is indicated in Table 3.5. This table reveals that 56% of respondents who reported that there was a tree planting program in their peasant association indicated also that there was no community forest in their peasant association, even though most of the tree planting was undertaken in the community forest. This finding shows that most of the farmers were actually planting in the community forest without being aware of it.

According to this study, neither the presence of a community forest nor the existence of a tree planting program in a peasant association made any difference

Table 3.5 Relationship Between the Community Forest
and the Tree Planting Program in Peasant Associations

Community Forest in PA	Tree Planting Program in PA		
	Present	Not Present	Number of Cases
Present	44%	9%	81
Not Present	56%	91%	149
Number of Cases	172	58	230

Note: Chi square significant at .001 level

in ameliorating the serious shortage of fuelwood. The majority of those (85%) who reported having a community forest had a serious wood shortage. Most of those (80%) who indicated the presence of a tree planting program in their peasant association also reported a serious shortage of fuelwood in their community. Not a single farmer indicated using the trees in the community forest. This is partly due to the fact that most of the trees were not ready for harvest. But it is also true that even in areas where the trees were ready for harvest, there was confusion among the peasant association leaders as to who should decide when and for what purposes they should be used. These findings are similar to a study done by Yeraswork Admassie, which found that none of the trees planted in the World Food Program catchment areas had been used by farmers and that farmers did not feel that the trees in community forests belonged to them.[14] Thus, community forests, as presently managed, are unlikely to be a major source of fuelwood.

Similar to the problems faced by individual farmers, no clear legal mandate empowers peasant associations to manage and utilize community forests. Members and leaders of peasant associations believed that community forests, in the final analysis, belonged to the government, and that the peasant association would not benefit from them. Thus, the involvement of the peasantry in community forest projects is essential if they are to be a reliable source of wood supply at the village level.

Another major drawback to the community forest program is that most interviewed farmers expressed their preference for an individual venture in tree planting over a communal one. This finding is supported by another study, which showed peasant selection of a poor site for a community forest vis-a-vis better land for individual planting, whenever they had the opportunity to do it by themselves.[15] Yet, the government effort concentrated on promoting communal ventures that hold little promise for the urgently needed increase in wood supply.

A village without hillside closure—a site of frequent flooding from mountain runoff, Gubalafto, Yeju.

Results of effective hillside closure under the Red Cross-funded Upper Mille and Cheleka Catchment Disaster Prevention Program, Tehulederie, Ambassel.

Area Closure: Reclamation of Degraded Land

After the 1984 famine, the need to preserve natural resources and stop the worsening degradation was urgently felt. Next to resettlement, area closure became one of the most important mechanisms to deal with these problems. According to the Ministry of Agriculture's guidelines for development agents, area closure is defined as "a protection system to improve land with degraded vegetation and/or soil through regeneration. No livestock is allowed to graze, and no human interference tolerated for 3-5 years, until an 80% natural grass cover is obtained."[16] The most common form in Wollo is hillside closure and it has become significant since 1980. The Ministry of Agriculture's zonal office for northeastern Ethiopia states that land under hillside closure in Wollo covers 66,536 hectares.[17]

This scheme has no cost and has shown promising results in a short period of time, particularly in areas where grazing on the hills is strictly prohibited. The study conducted by Marten Bendz specifically in the Red Cross catchment areas in Ambassel and Kalu awrajas shows that under hillside closure natural regeneration of grasses and bushes takes place rapidly within two to three years, soil erosion will be arrested after three to five years, and gullies and waterways will be halted after ten years.[18] A good example of the effects of hillside closure is observed when traveling from Dessie to Haik (the awraja town of Ambassel), and from Dessie to Kombolcha (the awraja town of Kalu). The hills on both sides of the road have been covered by bushes and naturally regenerated *Juniperus procera* since they were brought under hillside closure over fifteen years ago.

About half of the peasant associations covered under this study had area closures. Yet, over half of the interviewed farmers were unaware of their presence, just as they were unaware of a community forest in their peasant association. This provides further evidence of lack of participation among the peasantry in rehabilitation projects, that so greatly influence their lives and need their support.

Why would so many farmers not know about an area closure in their own peasant association? First, area closure was usually undertaken on the hills and the mountainous parts of the peasant association, which were seriously degraded. As a result, area closure tended to affect those who live nearby rather than those who were further away. Second, few farmers received benefits from area closure through the "cut and carry" system, which provides forage for livestock by cutting the grass under area closure twice a year, depending on rainfall. The majority of those who benefited from "cut and carry" were the ones who knew about the presence of area closure. Third, as with community forests, no systematic information was given to the farmers about the presence of area closure, and it was usually perceived as a government program.

An example of a peasant association where all five respondents knew that there was a hillside closure is the Chali peasant association (012) in Werebabo Wereda (Ambassel Awraja). Most of the respondents indicated that they practiced "cut and carry" and had a positive opinion about area closure. Discussions with peasant association leaders indicated that most farmers were allowed to harvest the grass under the hillside closure during the rainy season.

The major constraints in attaining the objective of area closures arise from their management and administration. In principle, area closure is to be established in close consultation with the peasant associations. In reality, peasant association leaders were instructed by extension agents that certain areas were designated for area closures after the decision was made. For example, two highland peasant associations (Akesta and Kindo) located in Legambo Wereda (Werehiminu Awraja) had hillside closures. Yet most of the interviewed farmers, including some executive committee members, did not know about them. All of the farmers indicated that there was a tree planting program on the hills of their peasant association, which they considered part of the government-run state forest. However, they were, in fact, hillside closures. Here, the administration and the management of the hillside closures, as in many places, were closely supervised by extension agents. To many in these peasant associations, hillside closure was a means of accumulating more land for the state forest, a major cause of the shortage of grazing land.[19]

The "cut and carry" system for areas under hillside closure was plagued by administrative problems. Peasant associations were supposed to decide on both who should use the grass and when it should be used. In principle, once the grass has fully recovered, farmers should cut the grass and use it for livestock feed and roof cover. Of twenty-seven peasant associations who had area closure, only eight (30%) practiced "cut and carry." Grass does not take a long time to recover, and there were several instances when grass under hillside closures was not being utilized even when it was ready for harvest (in the Bokokesa peasant association, Werebabo Wereda; in the Akesta peasant association, Legambo Wereda; and in Wobelo peasant association, Dessie Zurie Wereda). The peasant association that managed the "cut and carry" system was cautious in initiating the system until it got the go-ahead from extension agents. This was a major reason why the majority of the farmers who acknowledged the presence of area closure in their peasant associations did not practice "cut and carry."

Peasant opinion about area closure was for the most part negative, as exemplified by 66% of the respondents in the sample. Nearly all of the respondents with a negative opinion asserted that area closure resulted in a shortage of grazing area in their peasant associations. Most of these respondents did not practice "cut and carry." The minority of the respondents whose opinion about area closure was positive (29%) cited the availability of grass for livestock during the dry season, and most of them benefited from "cut and carry." Consequently, the presence of a "cut and carry" system is a significant factor in influencing the peasants' opinions about area closure. Why some have access to harvest grass under area closure while others do not is an important issue that needs further investigation.

The greatest constraint on the effectiveness and the expansion of area closure as a mechanism to rehabilitate and reclaim degraded land is lack of popular participation in its implementation and management. This problem was also observed by Marten Bendz, who sees the tenure issue regarding who controls and benefits from hillside closures to be the major obstacle in their management.[20] The absence of participation and clear guidelines on the utilization of the hillside led to the violation of the quarantine on hillside closure. Some of the interviewed peasant association leaders and extension agents admitted that some peasants had been found cutting grass and taking wood during the night. Like the peasants, the local guards, who were farmers themselves and paid little through the Food for Work Program had no motivation to enforce the quarantine.

Most peasants perceived area closure as another governmental intrusion in their lives and were resentful of the program. It is ironic that hillside closure resulted in a quick regeneration of grass when grazing was strictly forbidden on hills, while at the same time it invariably led to a serious shortage of grazing land. This inadvertently resulted in enormous livestock pressure on the most productive cropland, exposing it to more degradation. Without some mechanism that enlists peasant cooperation to reduce livestock size or change grazing patterns, hillside closure will have the unintended effect of rehabilitating marginal lands on the slopes while productive lands become degraded.

Furthermore, the threat of degradation for areas under area closure immediately after recovery comes mainly from livestock, as explained above. Yet little advice is given on controlled grazing and pasture management, both of which are important for the success of area closure. Any rehabilitation measure that affects livestock, such as area closure, has a devastating impact on the lives of the peasantry. Thus, it would be futile to implement such programs without their consultation and involvement. If area closure is to be successful in the reclamation of degraded land, the issue of grassroots participation on the part of peasant association leaders and members becomes once again paramount.

Notes

1. Paul Richards, "Ecological Change and the Politics of African Land Use," *African Studies Review*, Vol. 26, No. 2, June 1983, p. 50.

2. Piers Blaikie, *The Political Economy of Soil Erosion in Developing Countries*, New York: Longman, 1985. See also: Michael Watts, "Drought, Environment, and Food Security: Some Reflection on Peasants, Pastoralist and Commodization in Dryland West Africa," in Michael H. Glantz, *Drought and Hunger in Africa: Denying Famine a Future*, London: Cambridge University Press, 1987; Brian Spooner and H. S. Mann, *Desertification*

and Development: Dryland Ecology in Social Perspective, London: Academic Press, 1982.

3. Michael Watts, "Social Theory and Environmental Degradation" in Yehuda Gradus, *Desert Development: Man and Technology in Sparselands*, Boston: D. Reidel Publishing Company, 1985, p. 19.

4. Priscilla Reining, *Handbook on Desertification Indicators*, Washington, D.C.: American Association for the Advancement of Science, 1984.

5. Harold Dregne, *Desertification of Arid Lands*, New York: Harwood Academic Publishers, 1984.

6. Blaikie, *The Political Economy of Soil Erosion*, p. 15.

7. Yersawork Admassie, Mulugate Abebe, Markos Ezara, and J. Gay, *Report on the Sociological Survey and Sociological Considerations in Preparing a Development Strategy*, Ethiopian Highland Reclamation Study, Ministry of Agriculture, Addis Ababa, 1983, p. 40.

8. M. Constable and Members of the Ethiopian Highland Reclamation Study, *The Degradation of Resources and an Evalution of Actions to Combat It, Ethiopian Highlands Reclamation Study*, Working Paper 19, Ministry of Agriculture, Addis Ababa, December 1984, p. 40.

9. Data obtained from National Meteorological Services Agency, Addis Ababa, February 1989.

10. Hans Hurni, *Soil Conservation in Ethiopia: Guidelines for Development Agents*, Ministry of Agriculture, Addis Ababa, 1986, p. 9.

11. Data obtained from National Meteorological Services Agency, Addis Ababa, February 1989.

12. L. A. Lewis and L. Berry, *African Environment and Resources*, Boston: Unwin Hyman, 1988, pp. 142-145.

13. Micheal Arnold, "Community Forest," *Ambio: Journal of the Human Environment*, Volume 16, Number 2-3, 1987, pp. 122-128.

14. Yeraswork Admassie, *Impact and Sustainability of Activities for Rehabilitation of Forest, Grazing and Agricultural Lands*, United Nations World Food Program, Addis Ababa, September 1988, p. 41.

15. Markos Ezara and Kassahun Berhanu, *A Review of the Community Forestry Programme and an Evaluation of Its Achievements: A Socio-Economic Survey*, Swedish International Development Authority, Addis Ababa, January 1988, p. 89.

16. Hans Hurni, *Guidelines for Development Agents on Soil Conservation in Ethiopia*, Ministry of Agriculture, Addis Ababa, 1986, p. 70.

17. Data generated from the Ministry of Agriculture Zonal Office for North Eastern Ethiopia, Dessie, Wollo, February 1988.

18. Marten Bendz, *Hillside Closures in Wollo*, Rural Development Consultants AB, Vaxjo, Sweden, October, 1988, pp. 3-4.

19. In some peasant associations, controlled grazing was confused with area closure. Controlled grazing, continuous or rotational, limits the number of livestock able to graze on a certain area or totally restricts grazing during a certain period of time until the grass has recovered. It is a means of both improving pasture for livestock and preventing soil degradation. One of the few peasant associations that had controlled grazing (Debersoye, 060) was in Debersina Wereda, Borena Awraja. A diligent extension agent introduced controlled grazing to this relatively fertile peasant association. Animals were restricted

from this area during the rainy season when it is inundated by water. When the grass was ready to harvest, it was cut and taken for livestock feed. Hence, farmers practiced "cut and carry" under controlled grazing. After the rainy season when grass was scarce, livestock were allowed to graze in this area. Yet, the interviewed farmers in this section of the peasant association acknowledged it as an area closure. This confusion was due to the practice of "cut and carry" (usually not a main feature of controlled grazing) and to the restriction of grazing land. However, most of the farmers here said that this system improved the availability of grass during the long dry season, and gave credit to the extension agent who taught them about controlled grazing.

20. Bendz, *Hillside Closures in Wollo*, pp. 8-9.

4

Coping With Famine: Peasants Versus Government Responses

The history of famine in Ethiopia up until the nineteenth century is sketchy.[1] Mesfin Wolde-Mariam's book, *Rural Vulnerability to Famine in Ethiopia: 1958-1977*,[2] examines the impact of the four major famines in this century: (1) the Ethiopian famine of 1888-1892, caused by the devastation of oxen by rinderpest, which began in Eritrea and spread throughout the Ethiopian highlands and then southward into Somalia; (2) the Tigraye famine of 1958, in which about 100,000 people died; (3) the Wag and Lasta famine of 1966, which severely affected these two northern awrajas of Wollo; and (4) the Wollo famine of 1973, which affected most of Wollo (and parts of Tigraye), triggering the downfall of the Emperor Haile Selassie's government.[3]

Thanks to media exposure, no secrets were hidden about the 1984 famine. For the first time, the world was made aware of what the Ethiopian peasantry has suffered for centuries. The brutality of the famine and the size of the population affected was unparalleled in this century. Neither the indigenous survival mechanisms nor the government's efforts could handle a problem of such magnitude. Hence, relief centers, unknown in Ethiopia prior to the 1970s, became a major means of treating famine victims. Nothing dramatized the plight of the starving people to the world community as much as the relief centers in Bati and Korem during the 1984 famine. This publicity inspired human generosity and saved many lives. Yet, in that famine year alone, between half and three-quarters of a million people may have perished in Wollo.

To Wollo peasants, famine is as familiar as their villages. Nearly everyone in the sample witnessed at least two famine years in his lifetime; some saw three or four. The maximum number of famine years, five, was reported by a sixty-six-year-old farmer living in the lowland zone of Kobo Wereda (Raya & Kobo Awraja), Mendefra peasant association, which was among those identified as being severely affected by drought and in need of emergency food assistance. This farmer was at a relief center during the 1984/85 famine, in which he lost all of his livestock and one of his sons. For him, 1987 was another famine year. He had been receiving food assistance from the Relief and Rehabilitation Commission. Once a month, he travelled 10 kilometers to the wereda town of

Kobo, and carried 50 to 100 kilograms of flour on his shoulder back to his house.

The overwhelming number of respondents in this study (87%) reported that they were affected by the 1984/85 famine. "Affected" means having had a serious food shortage; experiencing the death of a son, a daughter, or a spouse; losing one's livestock; or fleeing one's community for rescue. The majority of the respondents (80%) received food assistance in various forms. The number of those who received food aid without being affected by famine was insignificant (6%). This figure indicates the relative success of food distribution to the famine victims. Further discussions with relief agents (both the government and voluntary agencies) confirmed that, for the most part, donated food reached those who needed it most. Thus, the allegation of systematic diversion of food aid by the government seemed to be unfounded.

Of those who received food assistance during the 1984/85 famine, the majority subsequently returned to their homes (82%), 16% joined relief centers, and 2% received assistance through Food for Work. Most of the respondents who joined relief centers were from Bati (Kalu Awraja), Habru Wereda (Yeju Awraja), and Kobo Wereda (Raya & Kobo Awraja), which also shows that the impact of the 1984 famine was more severe in northern than in western Wollo (comprised of Borena, Wereilu, and Werehiminu awrajas).

Accounts of the trauma and the tragedy of the 1984 famine and of the politics involved are extensively recounted by journalists, scholars, and Ethiopian and United Nations relief officials.[4] The focus of this study is to identify the factors that have made a difference in reducing vulnerability to famine at the village level, to point out the lessons learned from the 1984 famine, and to assess the actions taken by both peasants and government in combating future famine.

This study was conducted during a time when most of Wollo had a serious food shortage and some communities in northern Wollo were experiencing near-famine conditions. Farmers were asked whether they had some reserve food at the time of the interview. If their response was affirmative, they were then asked if it could last them until the next harvest (see Appendix 1). Those farmers who lacked enough reserve food to last them for three months were considered "vulnerable to famine" in this study. This is a relative measure of "vulnerability to famine" and indicates the imminent danger of starvation or serious food shortage, unless the situation is reversed in the immediate future. Thirty-five percent of the sampled farmers had no reserve food and were "vulnerable to famine." This finding is similar to that reported by the Ministry of Agriculture, which found that a third of the rural population in Wollo suffered from food shortage even in normal years. Of those who had some reserve food (65%), the majority (58%) had enough to last them until the next harvest, which was in six months; 31% had enough food to last for about three months, 8% had enough food for one year, and 3% had enough food to last for two years.

The socioeconomic aspects of famine are also discussed in Mesfin Wolde-

Mariam's book, which warns that famine is expanding to areas of the country that have not previously been affected. This is true in Wollo where famine has hit areas like Borena and Wereilu, which had previously been relatively self-sufficient in food. Mesfin's study sees famine as the "absolute absence of food" (commonly referred to as "sudden food availability decline") and examines its impact on humans, livestock, and the agricultural production system.[5]

The findings from this study indicate that famine is a "relative" phenomenon, whereby even in the same peasant association, some are devoured by famine while others are barely affected. The unequal impact of famine on communities and individuals is not exclusively due to political and economic forces, but also to ecological factors. To be sure, political and economic forces play a major role. For example, James McCann's study shows that one's access to oxen is a crucial factor in determining who survives under famine,[6] while Amartya Sen attributes famine to a sudden decline in the "distribution" of available food due to a failure in "exchange entitlement."[7] In seeing famine as the "relative absence of food," this study, however, does not accept an economic or political determinist view in explaining famine.

The questions that are of exceptional interest to this study are in regard to the characteristics of communities and individuals who appear less vulnerable in times of famine. A closer examination revealed that, with certain limits, the factors that enhance household food reserve in times of famine are livestock endowment, family size, access to irrigation, agroforestry practice, and off-farm employment.

Livestock Endowment: Sword or Ploughshare?

Livestock—a major cause of land degradation—are also a valuable asset in times of famine. Livestock are often used to purchase food, to pay taxes, and to finance household goods. As a result, even when farmers face chronic shortage of land, they would not like their size of stock to be reduced.

The 1984 famine had a devastating impact on livestock. In Wollo, the number of livestock (oxen, goats, and sheep) prior to the famine was estimated to be 5.2 million. In 1985, after a year of famine, the number of livestock was reported to be 3.4 million, and in 1986, 2.8 million.[8] In this study, 13% of the interviewed farmers had no livestock and attributed their loss to the 1984 famine. Serious shortage of pasture land and forage availability for livestock ruminants are a serious problem throughout the Ethiopian highlands, even in normal years. This shortage intensifies during drought years and, like food reserve, the peasants' livestock population diminishes rapidly.

During the fieldwork, several interesting observations emerged regarding the relationship between "vulnerability to famine" and livestock population. First, communities with a large amount of livestock suffered as much from

Figure 4.1 Household Vulnerability to Famine by Livestock Ownership

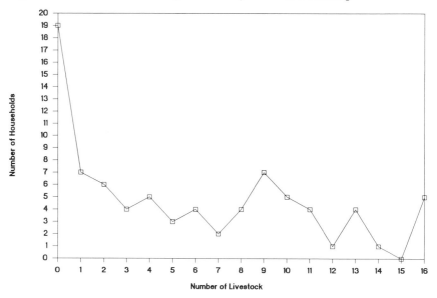

Figure 4.2 Household Vulnerability to Famine by Number of Oxen

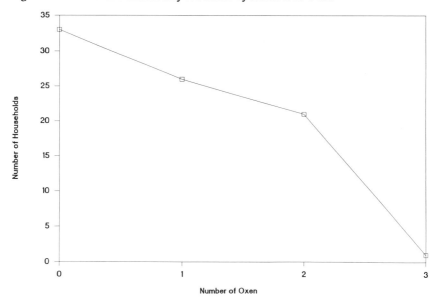

famine as those with a smaller livestock population. Bati Wereda (Kalu Awraja) had one of the highest livestock densities in Wollo, and yet it had one of the highest human and livestock death rates associated with the 1984/85 famine. The number of livestock ruminants in the three peasant associations selected in Bati were as follows: Chachatu (04) had 310 households and 3,287 livestock (an average of eleven livestock per household); Garero (07) had 533 households and 2,980 livestock (an average of six livestock per household); and Heto (014) had 394 households and 2,257 livestock (with an average of six livestock per household). Of the five farmers interviewed in each peasant association, four replied having no reserve food ("vulnerable to famine") in Chachatu and Heto, whereas only one reported having no reserve food in Garero.

It would seem that the number of livestock do not matter if a famine lasts for over a year, as did the 1984/85 famine. However, at the initial stage of famine, the number of livestock could contribute to the family reserve food as the family could purchase food by selling its livestock. The long- and short-term interplay in livestock population size is illustrated by the experience of one of the interviewed farmers in the Chachatu peasant association (04) who lived 12 kilometers from the town of Bati. This fifty-eight-year-old farmer lost forty cattle, forty-five sheep, twenty-five goats, and three camels during the 1984 famine. Like so many others in this association who lost most of their livestock, he managed to survive the prolonged famine year through food aid he received from the Red Cross in Bati.

At the same time, this farmer was the only one among the five interviewed farmers in this peasant association who had enough reserve food to last him for three to six months during the initial stage of the 1984/85 famine. With twenty-three livestock ruminants he had the largest number of livestock among the interviewed farmers in this peasant association (the others had thirteen, six, four, and two livestock ruminants). These figures indicate that the disparities in livestock possession among households (which was pervasive) *within* a peasant association are a more important factor in explaining "vulnerability to famine" than the disparities *between* peasant associations. Like the farmer in the Chachatu peasant association, farmers with a large livestock population can sell some of them to buy food in the anticipation of famine. Hence, livestock endowment contributes to the household availability of reserve food, at least in the initial stages of a famine. As the famine continues, then, the livestock population size becomes insignificant.

Although no significant statistical relationship is observed between livestock ownership and "vulnerability to famine," Figure 4.1, presents two somewhat contradictory indications. On the one hand, livestock ownership does matter; of the twenty-nine households that owned no livestock, nineteen were "vulnerable to famine." Also a *considerable* number of households with a large number of livestock were also "vulnerable to famine." On the other hand, a large livestock population does not make one immune to severe food shortage in times of famine. Several cases were observed in the severely famine-affected weredas of Kobo and Werebabo, in which a large number of livestock did not guarantee adequate food reserve for a household. When famine grips a community, livestock depreciate and local buyers are not readily available. Thus, livestock do not automatically command the power to purchase food. Others who had many livestock and who were still vulnerable to famine lived in the Delanta Wereda (Wadela Delanta Awraja),where most farmers rely on sheep-raising to supplement their income. This awraja is rather isolated, with poor infrastructure and a limited outlet to markets outside the awraja. Hence, prices for livestock are very low in normal years and much lower in times of crisis.

This study reveals that what is important in securing enough food to last until the next harvest is not so much a large number of livestock, but rather a minimal number that includes at least one ox (see Figure 4.2). Of the fifty-one households with no oxen, thirty-three were "vulnerable to famine." Oxen used for ploughing are the single most desired livestock in peasant agriculture. Of the farmers who had access to oxen, 76% had enough reserve food to last until the next harvest, while 24% of those lacking oxen had enough reserve food. Thus, a significant statistical relationship is observed between access to oxen and "vulnerability to famine." This is similar to a finding of another study, which found access to oxen to be a crucial factor in determining who starved or survived in northern Shewa during the 1984 famine year.[9]

Moreover, the role of livestock as a risk-averting mechanism in times of famine was evidenced in Bati Wereda, one of the areas hardest hit by the 1987 drought. Most of the farmers interviewed had no food reserve; consequently, they registered to receive relief assistance. The few that had reserve food in these weredas have a considerably larger number of livestock than the others, and had been selling their livestock to purchase food.

Table 4.1 Relationship Between Family Size and Vulnerability to Famine

Family Size	Percentage Vulnerable to Famine	Percentage Not Vulnerable to Famine	Number of Respondents
2	30	70	10
3	6	94	18
4	25	75	28
5	39	61	41
6	35	65	55
7	38	62	39
8	47	53	17
9	58	42	12
10	50	50	10

Note: Chi Square significant at 0.1 level

In summary, this study signifies that livestock endowment per se does not make peasant households immune from famine in times of drought. Yet, those with no livestock were clearly more vulnerable to famine. Access to oxen is an important factor that greatly reduces households' vulnerability to famine. In an attempt to deal with famine, ensuring the availability of oxen is more important than increasing the number of livestock. In light of the prominent role livestock play in land degradation (as discussed above), the provision of oxen to peasants without increasing the overall number of livestock is a delicate issue that will be dealt with below.

Family Size: Burden or Resource?

The threat of the uncontrolled population growth to cultivable land size and soil fertility was discussed earlier. This study also indicates that family size significantly influences the amount of food reserve a family has for consumption.

Table 4.1 shows that with all factors being equal, a considerable number of respondents with less than four members in their households had enough food to last them until next harvest than those exceeding four members. This reveals a significant statistical relationship between household size and availability of food.

An example of this is seen in the Kelo peasant association (02), located in the lowland area of Eseyegola Wereda (Kalu Awraja), which was seriously affected by drought and most residents were registering to receive food when this study was conducted. Of the five households interviewed in this peasant association, two of the farmers reported having enough food to last them until the next harvest. These farmers had considerably smaller family size than the rest of the farmers in this peasant association. One of these farmers was a sixty-six-year-old man who lived with his thirty-year-old wife. This farmer was married four times and had eleven children. Only one of his children was alive, the other ten having died of famine (the largest number of children reported to have died of famine). He had lived through three famines in his lifetime. The first one was the 1973 famine which took the lives of six of his children, all under ten years old. As the 1973 famine continued, three of his children died between 1974 and 1975 due to famine-related illnesses. The 1984 famine took the life of one of his children. His remaining son lived on his own in the nearby small town. Although this farmer had no livestock, he asserted that it was not that difficult to look after his young wife, although who really looked after whom was questionable.

The second farmer who had enough food to last until the next harvest in the Kelo peasant association was a sixty-year-old farmer who had four members in his household. Like most in this peasant association, he was Muslim, but was only married once—to the same woman he was living with at the time. He had seven children, but four died due to illness—reportedly unrelated to famine.

Two of his children lived with him and were over the age of fifteen. He acknowledged that both of them greatly assisted him in farming, which suggests that children over a certain age are also contributors to household food reserves rather than mere consumers swelling the dependency burden that is frequently observed in rural Ethiopia. The repeated assertion made in the development literature that children are a major means of security during old age is true. They are at the same time, however, a source of intense strain on the meager resource of rural households in Ethiopia. Hence, reducing family size, an important policy objective for Ethiopia, has to also be approached from the broader perspective of improving the conditions of peasant households.

Small Irrigation Schemes: Making a Difference

Irrigated land in Wollo is like an oasis in the desert. It ensures the availability of food from the end of one harvesting season to the beginning of another. The irrigation methods in all cases depend on the gravitational flow of water and involve the diversion of rivers or streams by digging a waterway from nearby hills, mountains, or elevated areas close to the peasant association.

Of the forty-six peasant associations selected, fourteen (30%) have some kind of irrigation scheme. Not every member has access to the irrigated land. In fact, in two of the peasant associations in Ambassel Awraja (Tehulederie Wereda), only members of producer cooperatives had access to the irrigation. In the twelve remaining peasant associations with irrigation schemes, most farmers were not benefiting from irrigation—only twenty farmers (representing 9% of the sample) benefitted. In Wollo, irrigated land covers about 1% of cultivated land. The areas under irrigation are small—all below five hectares, and the total amount of irrigated land is about 7,288 hectares, 45% of them concentrated in Raya & Kobo (with 1,683 hectares) and in Yeju awrajas (with 1,604 hectares).[10] The twenty farmers who were using irrigation in this sample lived in Yeju, Raya & Kobo, Kalu, Borena, and Dessie Zurie awrajas.

The major problem of gravitational flow irrigation in all regions was unequal access to irrigated land. Why did some farmers have access while others, who live in the same peasant association, did not?

1. Most of the irrigation schemes divert streams and small rivers and are too small to reach every plot. Even when, as in some cases, the quantity of water may be adequate, the topography of the peasant association and the location of the individual plots, scattered at different elevations, pose major constraints.

2. The water flowing down from the main channel is received in differing quantities based on the location of the farm. Therefore, the farmers that benefit were usually on the lower slope, in the valley where most of the water is distributed, or had plots closer to the stream or river that was being diverted.

In the absence of technology, it is a formidable task to transport water upwards and downwards to areas far from the source. Consequently, irrigated land covers a tiny portion of the total land in the peasant associations.

3. Individual farmers who had access to irrigated land acquired it through inheritance. Some farmers with no irrigated land (as was the case in the Weyniyie peasant association in Yeju Awraja) actually rented a small portion from the farmers who had irrigated land.

4. Most of the irrigated land belonged to members of producer cooperatives. Individual farmers were asked more and more frequently to relinquish their irrigated plots if they did not want to join producer cooperatives.

In the sample, nearly all of the farmers who used irrigation had enough reserve food until the next harvest (approximately six months), indicating a statistically significant relationship between the two variables. In fact, of the sampled farmers who indicated having enough food for a year (8%), a third used irrigation.

Given the capriciousness of nature, access to irrigated land in the life of a Wollo peasant is like a pathway to a promised land. In every peasant association, either in the lowland or the highland, those who had irrigated land were a source of envy to those who lacked it. Every effort was made to own a piece of irrigated land, even if it meant joining the unpopular collective farm. In the Weyniyie peasant association (016), in Gubalafto Wereda (Yeju Awraja), for instance, a producer cooperative was established in 1985 on 60 hectares of irrigated land. Contrary to the decline in membership often observed in producer cooperatives, Weyniyie experienced an increase from 300 family heads in 1985, when it was established, to 400 family heads in 1987. The major reason for the increase in membership was undoubtedly the access to irrigated land.

Moreover, two central issues emerged in examining the role of irrigation at the village level. First was the contrast between a peasant association that had irrigation and one that did not. Second was the remarkable difference between those with and those without access to irrigation in the same peasant association. It was startling to conduct an interview with a farmer on an irrigated homestead in lush green surroundings with bananas, sugar cane, and vegetable gardens, and in the same peasant association, later that day, see livestock browsing the dry sorghum field of another farmer who had no access to irrigated land.

In one of the peasant associations, we saw a rare sight: oxen ploughing in November, in the middle of the dry season. This was in Borena Awraja (Debersina Wereda) 10 kilometers west of the wereda town of Mekanselam, at the Debersoye peasant association (060), on irrigated land. The classic example of diversion of a river for the purpose of irrigation was seen in this scenic peasant association that descends gently, like a stream, from an altitude of 2,600 to 2,300 meters. Diverted water flowed continuously through the hills to cover more area in the valley and lower slope, which are suited for cultivation. The water was then apportioned to individual plots extending from the lower slope to the valley. The irrigated land was relatively large (5 hectares) and, unlike in many peasant associations, was partitioned fairly among its members, partly because they have 50 years experience managing irrigation in this community.

In this peasant association, all of the interviewed farmers except one indicated that they had enough reserve food to last them for at least six months until the next harvest. (It is noteworthy that the two farmers who had enough reserve food for a year had small irrigated plots.) In most cases, irrigated plots did not exceed a half hectare. In this peasant association, those with an irrigated plot cultivated onions, peppers, spices, and vegetables several times a year, bringing in a constant flow of cash income. They also cultivated such cereals as teff, wheat, and sorghum on the other less fertile plots for family consumption. This was one of the few peasant associations where most of the farmers interviewed were neither affected by nor received food assistance during the 1984/85 famine.

In the Girana peasant association (018) located in the lowland zone of Habru Wereda (Yeju Awraja), due to the lack of a rainy season in 1987, the vast part of this peasant association was covered by stunted sorghum, completely abandoned for livestock grazing. Only the irrigated section, dominated by the members of the producer cooperative, had a harvest that season. Of the farmers interviewed in this peasant association, only two who used irrigation reported having reserve food, while others with no access to irrigation had scarcely any food and could face starvation. One of the farmers admitted that, had it not been for the harvest he got from his irrigated plot of less than 0.25 hectare, he would have had no harvest, like most of the others in this peasant association. This farmer lost most of his irrigated land to the producer cooperative; in spite of this, he had no intention of joining it.

Gravitational irrigation can be an unreliable source of water in the absence of rainfall or when there is excessive loss of water due to runoff or erosion in the highland areas. Hence, the afforestation of the highlands where the major rivers and streams originate is important in maintaining a water supply for gravitational irrigation projects. The irrigation potential of the highlands of Werehiminu, Wereilu, Borena, Wadela Delanta, and Dessie Zurie (commonly referred to as western Wollo) was totally untapped. The field investigation suggests that these awrajas appeared to have greater potential for gravitational irrigation than Yeju and Raya & Kobo (referred to as northern Wollo), which had considerably more irrigated land than those awrajas in western Wollo. Several of the peasant associations we visited in western Wollo were close to streams that are tributaries of the Nile River and could be used for irrigation with some effort and imagination.[11] Thus, developing an irrigation scheme in many highlands of western Wollo needs to be considered seriously by policymakers, since the findings of this study ascertain that small irrigation schemes play an indisputable role in both substantially reducing the vulnerability to famine and in controlling the microenvironment.

Agroforestry: Surviving on Marginal Land

A useful and objective approach to examining the role of agroforestry was given by P. K. R. Nair and E. Fernandes at the International Council for Research in Agroforestry. Agroforestry was defined as "land use systems and practices where woody perennials (trees, shrubs, palms, bamboos, etc.) are deliberately used on the same land management unit as agricultural crops and/or animals, either in some form of spatial arrangement or in a temporal sequence."[12] The important elements to note in agroforestry, regardless of its definition, are: (1) the dominant feature is not the forests, but rather the farming system under which the forest operates. Agroforestry complements the existing farming system; (2) the forest and other perennials interact with crops and livestock systems to provide both environmental protection and economic benefit; and (3) it can optimize land use with the least possible amount of degradation.

Small-scale irrigation employing gravitational flow is easy to operate, Weyniyie, Yeju.

Very little is known about agroforestry in Ethiopia. The few communities that practiced it in Wollo used the system without knowing that they were practicing agroforestry. Of the sampled peasant associations, only three had a traditional agroforestry system. Two types of agroforestry were identified. The first involved the integration of a cash crop (coffee, *chat* and *gesho*) with the farming system, which produced cereal for consumption; the second involved fruit crops. Irrespective of the type of agroforestry practiced, most of the respondents in these peasant associations had enough reserve food until the next harvest. In the vast lowland of Eseyegola Wereda (Kalu Awraja), where scattered acacia trees and dry sorghum stalk fields abounded, two peasant associations that practiced agroforestry had landscapes unlike any other in this wereda. These peasant associations (Dinkeye Gelana and Dinkeye Gobensa), located in the village of Rike with a hilly, medium altitude zone, had spectacular forests on the upper slope, coffee and *chat* around the homesteads, and cereal cultivation on the lower slopes and in the valleys. Most of the respondents in these peasant associations had reserve food, regardless of their disappointing harvesting season. A considerable number of the peasants had attributed their food reserves to their coffee and *chat* trees (the leaves of the *chat* tree are commonly chewed among Muslims and are a form of mild drug), which provided them with some income to purchase cereal during the crisis. A seventy-six-year-old farmer, the oldest man in the sample, was a typical representative. There were six members in his household, and he owned a total of one hectare in three different plots. His main plot of one-half hectare around his homestead was allocated to coffee and *gesho* (a tree used in the fermentation of the Ethiopian beverages *teje* and *tela*). On the rest of his plot he cultivated teff, wheat, and maize. This farmer indicated that he had enough food to last him for six months—until *belg* harvest in June. Even if that harvest failed, he asserted rather self-assuredly, pointing to his coffee tree, he would be able to sell some of his coffee and buy food that would last him for a few more months.

In Rike, even in years of below-average rainfall in the *belg* or *meher* seasons there is relatively more moisture available to sustain limited cropping. This is because the forests and perennial crops that are on the ground throughout the year significantly add to the high biomass cover. Dense vegetative cover protects the soil from erosion, recycles nutrients, and helps maintain moisture content in soil reducing crop failures in times of drought.

The other peasant association with extensive agroforestry, involving the cultivation of fruit crops (bananas, sugar cane, and oranges) around the homestead and cereal cultivation on other nonirrigated plots, was Weyniyie, Yeju Awraja, Gubalafto Wereda. There was a serious land shortage in this peasant association, which had about 800 hectares (not all of which were cultivable, particularly the land on the upper slope) and 1,530 members. The average landholding per household was about one-half hectare. Cereal production in a normal year was primarily used for family consumption. The income these farmers got from fruit crops assisted them in paying taxes, buying household items, and enhancing their overall ability to cope in times of famine.

The development of agroforestry in Wollo is of particular importance, since

Agroforestry—cultivation of fruit crops such as banana and sugar cane around the homestead, Weyniyie, Yeju.

A community that practices agroforestry, growing cereals on the terrace and coffee and fruit trees on the hill, Rike, Kalu.

most of the land is vulnerable to erosion due to its rugged topography and there are different ecological zones even within a peasant association. In Wollo, agroforestry has great potential for reducing vulnerability to famine by providing additional food and cash sources, meeting fuelwood requirements, and increasing vegetative cover that would prevent erosion and maintain soil fertility.

Rural Employment: Rarely an Option

Apart from agriculture, there is no source of employment to supplement income in the Ethiopian highlands. The closest thing to off-farm employment was the case of the handful of farmers, comprising 3% of the sampled farmers, who in addition to farming, wove clothes for rural households. Most of these farmers, irrespective of the ecological zones in which they lived, had some reserve food. Nearly every farmer interviewed in four of the selected peasant associations in Kobo Wereda had no reserve food. One of the respondents, who reported having food that could last him three months, was a part-time weaver in the Aradom peasant association (011). He was fifty-six-years-old and had three children. One of his daughters, who was married at age twelve, was fourteen and lived with him and her husband. He had neither an ox nor any kind of livestock, as they all died during the 1984 famine. Yet, in return for weaving clothes for those who had oxen, he gained access to oxen to plough his land. Since the 1984 famine, he spent more of his time weaving clothes than farming, and sold his clothes to small traders in nearby towns. This trade enabled him to earn some money for food during the famine year. A similar case was also found in Wadela Delanta Awraja (Goshmeda peasant association) where a part-time weaver asserted that he was able to survive through the 1984 famine by migrating to the nearest town in Delanta and weaving clothes until the end of that famine year.

Peasant Response to the 1984/85 Famine

The scars of the 1984/85 famine were everywhere in the villages of Wollo. No one was untouched by the tragedy. If it was not a close family member who died or left for resettlement, it was a distant relative. If it was not a relative, it was a friend or an acquaintance. In spite of the scars, when asked about the impact of the 1984/85 famine, the majority of the farmers showed no visible distress. What is remarkable is the resilient nature of the peasantry; their ability to bounce back to their normal activities after a year of chaos and destruction. Dessalegn Rahmato summarized his own experience by saying, "Wollo may be a land of famine but let no one say it is a land of sorrows."[13]

The indigenous survival mechanism in times of famine—particularly in the absence of external aid—is well documented in Rahmato's study *Famine and*

Survival Strategies: A Case Study from Northeast Ethiopia. The author has given a detailed account of what he called "anticipatory and crisis survival strategies" based on fieldwork at Ambassel Awraja in Wollo.[14] The objective of this study is not so much to stress survival strategies, but rather to assess the lessons learned and the actions being undertaken to prevent future famine. This study will specifically attempt to address the following questions:

1. In what ways did the 1984 famine significantly change peasants' actions and behaviors at the individual level?
2. Did peasant associations take some measures to assist in dealing with such crises collectively in the future?

It should be stated at the outset that there are two forces that undermine peasants' actions in dealing with famine. The first is structural causes, that is to say, the political and institutional forces under which peasant agriculture operates. The second is natural causes—the rainfall pattern, which peasants consider the primary factor in crop failure for all the famine years they have seen.

Peasants are the most peripheral group in the power structure of Ethiopia. In spite of the rhetoric of the present "Marxist" government, peasant influence on government policy is insignificant. Peasant institutions, established to serve and protect their interest following the 1975 Agrarian Reform, have retrogressed each year to become more and more the organ of government policy—a policy whose priority is not exactly combating famine. As Mesfin Wolde-Mariam succinctly put it, peasants, who constitute the bulk of Ethiopia's population, "never had any significance in terms of power and influence. This fact must be included as one of the most important aspects of the problem of famine in Ethiopia and its increasing frequency and magnitude."[15]

Shortage of rain is the primary reason to which peasants attribute their misfortune during a famine year. While this study was in progress, Kobo Wereda was severely affected by famine and relief operations were underway. The largest number of people in the sample who were "vulnerable to famine" were found in Kobo Wereda. The amount of rainfall from 1976 to 1988 in the town of Kobo (the wereda town of Kobo Wereda) is presented in Table 4.2. The rainfall station in Kobo was within 25 square kilometers of the peasant associations selected in Kobo Wereda and all were located in the lowland areas. Hence, the data presented in Table 4.2 are most likely to be representative of the amount of rainfall received in the areas covered in Kobo Wereda under this study. Yet, meteorological data have to be taken cautiously. The National Meteorological Service has no rainfall station in many places in Ethiopia. In such cases, the Ministry of Agriculture, the Institute of Agricultural Research, and other government agencies in the area collect the data and pass it on to the National Meteorological Service. As a result, there is ambiguity in the data given by

Table 4.2 Monthly Rainfall in Kobo Station, Kobo Wereda (millimeters)

Months	Years											
	1977	78	79	80	81	82	83	84	85	86	87	88
January	16.6	2.1	89.2	0.5	0.0	16.8	5.1	0.0	4.4	0.0	0.0	37.5
February	3.9	18.62	106	15.7	NA	19.3	0.0	0.0	34.2	1.0	57.7	
March	88.1	40.9	28.9	23.7	NA	38.9	67.3	3.1	59.8	10.1	94.7	5.3
April	57.0	42.3	10.9	53.8	NA	80.3	88.2	16.0	76.7	73.0	51.2	44.8
May	123.5	35.9	78.4	26.0	9.7	28.2	114.7	0.0	44.3	91.4	127.8	0.3
June	5.7	4.6	17.0	27.7	0.0	0.0	24.5	0.0	5.5	75.3	6.8	13.1
July	156.0	236.3	149.0	199.2	256.1	44.1	25.5	8.2	0.0	134.3	15.9	193.4
August	237.0	76.3	181.2	220.1	277.9	174.8	73.6	14.3	133.2	225.5	116.2	166.3
September	66.7	27.5	110.6	47.3	65.9	124.5	27.3	29.0	101.3	90.3	37.1	100.4
October	0.0	12.2	46.0	32.7	45.6	18.5	24.2	0.0	8.8	0.0	64.5	22.2
November	6.9	12.0	0.0	0.0	0.0	0.0	2.3	6.2	0.0	0.0	0.0	0.0
December	4.0	17.6	15.1	0.0	3.7	0.0	0.0	28.6	0.0	26.5	0.0	0.0
Total	765.4	526.3	832.3	646.7	658.9	645.4	452.7	105.4	468.2	727.4	571.9	583.3

Source: National Meteorological Services Agency and Ministry of Agriculture Wereda Office in Kobo, Wollo[16]

various agencies for the same year and months under consideration.

The most important activities that determine bumper harvest or total crop failure in peasant agriculture is the rainfall during the short rainy season between the months of February and April (*belg*), and during the long rainy season between the middle of June and early September (*meher*). The rain during the *meher* season is supposed to be more than during the *belg* season.

Table 4.2 suggests that the two most recent famines in Kobo Wereda, the 1984 and 1987 famines, have a great deal to do with the failure of rain during the *belg* and *meher* seasons in 1984 and the variability in the rainfall patterns in 1987. The failure of rain during the *belg* and *meher* season is evidenced in Table 4.1 as lowest amount of rainfall is recorded in 1984 between February and April which was followed by another lowest rainfall between June and August. The total annual rainfall in 1984 (105.4 millimeters) was also substantially lower than any of the years presented in Table 4.1. Hence, the severe shortage of rain, particularly in both the *belg* and *meher* season, could result in the collapse of peasant agricultural production and widespread famine as witnessed in Kobo during the 1984 famine.

On the other hand, examining the 1987 rainfall data in Table 4.2 shows that there was enough rain in March and April in Kobo to enable farmers to plant crops during the *belg* season. Most farmers in Kobo Wereda, however, did not have the tradition of cultivating during the *belg* season and relied heavily on flooded water from the highlands of Lasta Awraja for *meher* cultivation. This was confirmed by the extension agents working in Kobo Wereda who had began disseminating information among farmers about the importance of *belg* cultivation. A few of the interviewed farmers in Kobo indicated cultivating teff during the *belg* season recently.

Another factor that may have contributed to crop failure in Kobo in 1987 was mostly likely the variability in rainfall pattern during the *meher* season rather than shortage of rain. According to one of the interviewed farmers who lived in the Mendefra peasant association (08), 9 kilometers from the town of Kobo, the problem with the 1987 *meher* rain was that it came too late and in such great quantity that it destroyed a few of the crops that had grown. In examining the daily rainfall data collected by the Ministry of Agriculture in Kobo, there seems to be some validity to this farmer's account. All the rain in the month of June and July came on two days (June 10 and July 30), and nearly three-quarters of the rain in the month of August came in the first week. Heavy rain damages plant stock and affects its maturation. In particular, teff, a major crop in this area, is sensitive to heavy rain as its fine and weed-like stalks are unable to withstand it.

What lessons had peasants learned from the 1984/85 famine, and what actions are they taking to deal with future famine? In regard to the first question, 85% of the farmers interviewed said the 1984/85 famine had changed their behavior. The majority of these respondents (60%) said that they were more frugal than before; they did not spend lavishly on weddings, mourning, and other festivities. It is difficult to know whether peasants meant what they said, or whether it was an easier response to give when they were suddenly put on the spot as to what they were doing to help themselves. It may be true that they were spending less on festivities, but the generous nature of the peasantry appeared to be intact. When I was working in Wollo, a guest could not leave the house of a peasant without being offered something to eat or drink, even during a time of scarcity. Giving, in the norms of the peasantry, represents the act of being alive.

After the 1984 famine, a good number (22%) of the respondents ploughed, prepared the fields, and planted each time it rained. They no longer waited for the traditional planting season. Wollo was witnessing not only the absence of rainfall at the expected time, but also its presence at unexpected times. For example, December is usually one of the driest months of the dry season and is the peak of the harvesting time. The amount of rainfall in millimeters for the month of December in Debersina Wereda (at Soye, close to the wereda town of Mekanselam, Borena Awraja) in 1983 was 1.8, in 1984 was 0.0, in 1985 was 0.0, in 1986 was 1.6, in 1987 was 13.9, and in 1988 was 0.0.[17] As the data indicate, December 1987 had relatively excessive precipitation. We were witnesses to this heavy rainfall that drenched many parts of the Borena Awraja in the first week of December. As a result, relief trucks going to Sayent Wereda (to the town of Ajibar) were halted. We were also stranded by this storm in the middle of our journey from Mekanselam to Ajibar (50 kilometers of dirt road). Thanks to the peasants who helped push our car through a nearly impenetrable mud slide and up one of the steepest slopes in the area, we arrived safely in Ajibar.

This experience underscores the fact that increasing variability in rainfall patterns adversely affects food production. For instance, as a result of the unexpected rainfall in Borena Awraja, those who were still collecting and storing their harvest suffered a great loss. Thus, the ploughing and planting of crops each time it rains is an appropriate response by the peasants. After this year, collecting and storing grains immediately after a harvest should be of vital importance to many, as well.

Some farmers in the sample (8%) reported that they did not sell as much during normal years as they had prior to the 1984/85 famine. These farmers were located in Delanta, Bati, Gubalafto, Ambassel, Kutaber and Dessie Zurie weredas. An example of such a farmer lived in the Gaberiel peasant association (030) in Gubalafto Wereda (Yeju Awraja). This forty-year-old man had six household members and three-quarters of his land was located on a marginal plot on the upper slope. He indicated that his house was about 8 kilometers from the nearest market place in Woldeyia, and he had access to market if he wanted to sell his produce. But he sold only a small portion of his harvest, to enable him to pay taxes and buy other essential household items, and kept the rest for family consumption because of his experience with the 1984 famine. Some of these farmers also reported that they sold their cattle to buy grain at a postharvest price, when it is cheaper, and saved it until they were sure they were out of a crisis.

Other reported changes in the behavior of farmers as the result of the 1984/85 famine year include:

1. Cultivating during the *belg* in areas that were traditionally cultivated only during the *meher*. These farmers (in Kobo, Debersina, and Sayent weredas) felt that cropping during *belg* helped them in increasing production. It had at the same time resulted in the reduction of fallow and pasture land.

2. Rearing livestock, particularly goats, which are resilient to drought. These farmers were found in the Goshmeda peasant association (032), Delanta Wereda, Chachatu peasant association (04), Bati Wereda, and Kesekebele peasant association (038), Habru Wereda. Most people in these peasant associations were severely affected by the 1987 famine. These farmers, who were rearing livestock to supplement their income, indicated having enough food to last them for three to six months; hence they were some of the few farmers that were not "vulnerable to famine" when this study was in progress. Although there is no statistical relationship between livestock rearing and "vulnerability to famine," it is plausible that those who are able to supplement their income from livestock and livestock products are likely to have more access to food reserve.

3. Cultivating vegetable gardens with spices, onions, peppers, and vegetables for cash income. These farmers were found in the medium altitude

peasant associations in all the weredas of Borena Awraja, in Gubalafto Wereda (Yeju Awraja), Tehulederie Wereda (Ambassel Awraja), and Kutaber Wereda (Dessie Zurie Awraja). Nearly all of the farmers who devoted part of their land near their homestead to vegetable gardens indicated having enough reserve food to last them until the next harvest. In addition to cash crops, some were also planting sweet potatoes, a drought resistant root crop that had not been planted prior to the 1984 famine.

4. Being involved in petty trading with small towns and villages to supplement income. These farmers lived in the Negusgalie peasant association (03) in Kobo Wereda, in the Dana peasant association (01) in Habru Wereda (Yeju Awraja), and the Chali peasant association (012) in Werebabo Wereda (Ambassel Awraja). The farmer in Kobo Wereda carefully selected the markets where some food or household items were cheap, and resold them in another market where they were expensive. He went to the highland of Lasta Awraja where he bought sheep cheaply and resold them in Kobo where they were relatively expensive. The farmers in Habru and Werebabo bought household items from the nomadic Afars, who roam freely between Ethiopia and Djibouti, and sold them to other farmers and small town traders. This trading takes place in the dry season and all the farmers started it after the 1984 famine. All three farmers who were involved in such trading indicated having enough reserve food.

5. Building better storage facilities to protect against rats and rodents. The farmer who gave this response lived in one of the most inaccessible peasant associations, Wetege (017), 35 kilometers from the Wadela Delanta awraja town Wegeltena. His most serious problem was postharvest loss due to rats and insects. The little he harvested during the 1984 famine was primarily lost because of bad storage facilities. Since then he constructed a new storage facility which stood sufficiently higher from the ground and with a tin cover on top to prevent rats from climbing up.

Following the 1984 famine, the major collective activity in the attempt to deal with famine has been the planting of trees. (As discussed above, tree planting was undertaken by the peasant associations in the community forest, and has its own problems.) Besides tree planting, there was very little communal effort to prevent future famine at the village level. For example, none of the peasant associations or service cooperatives had grain storage facilities, which are the most effective means of surviving in times of famine. This lack of communal effort seems ironic, considering that the government prides itself on being socialist. The only noteworthy collective effort was the construction of ponds by peasant associations. Huge pits were dug in the open fields to store water during the rainy season; this water could be used during the dry season when water is in short supply. Most of these ponds were constructed in Raya & Kobo Awraja (76 ponds) and Wereilu Awraja (30 ponds), which were considered to have high potential for development (known as "surplus-producing areas").[18] The Ministry of Agriculture's zonal office, through its extension agents, was making a concerted effort to promote this action. Due to the concentration of extension agents in surplus-producing weredas, most of the ponds that were constructed were limited to this zone. The major problem with the construction of ponds was the unanticipated outbreak of malaria that plagued many of the lowland areas where such construction had taken place. Most of the ponds did not have cement covers; they also lacked any means of filtering floods and sewage, and were therefore unsanitary. There was a bumper harvest in many parts of Wollo in 1988, particularly in Kobo and Eseyegola weredas (around Kemissie). But many farmers died in these areas due to malaria. In fact, many have argued that in these lowland areas, malaria in 1988 took more lives than famine in 1987. The government did not admit to the presence of malaria in Ethiopia. Be that as it may, it is difficult to rule out the unsanitary conditions of ponds as a factor in the unprecedented spread of malaria we witnessed during the fieldwork in Kobo, Bati, and Eseyegola weredas.

Government Policy in Dealing with Famine

Military expenditure consumes a major part of Ethiopia's economy. A study showed that defense spending (Ministry of Defense) rose from 105.8 million birr in 1973/74 to 1.5 billion birr in 1988/89. The share of defense in total expenditure rose from 18% in the early 1970s to 50% in 1988.[19] This was largely due to the escalating war against the secessionist movement in Eritrea and another Marxist rebel movement in the Tigraye region.

The tragedy of the civil war in Ethiopia is that it affects the regions that are ravaged by frequent famine such as Eritrea, Tigraye, and part of Wollo. In these regions, nothing is as devastating to peasant agriculture as war—an issue apparently dismissed by both the government and the rebel liberation leaders. The liberation of people in these regions, with the most fragile ecosystem in Ethiopia, should begin with ending the specter of war, which is fueled by regional and local politics. It is beyond the scope of this study to grapple with the effect of the war on famine. But it is certain that the Ethiopian peasants, irrespective of the region they come from, suffer the brunt of the war.

With this issue in the background, this study will examine the actions of the Ministry of Agriculture, which has the greatest responsibility in designing preventative measures to deal with famine. The specific questions it will attempt to answer are whether the Ministry of Agriculture had taken specific steps to deal with the recurring famine in this region, and if the Ministry's extension agents were imparting advice to peasants on ways to avert or cope with famine in the future. Major agricultural policies do not originate in the Ministry, but rather in the ruling politburo of the Ethiopian Worker's Party. The technocrats in the Ministry find themselves implementing controversial policies, which, they often privately admitted, are bound to fail. With this in mind, the impact of the policies enunciated by the Ministry of Agriculture to attain food self-sufficiency and to combat famine in Wollo will be briefly reviewed.

After the 1984 famine the Ethiopian government proposed a national policy to attain food self-sufficiency through dramatic increase in food production in selected surplus-producing weredas. This would involve the concentration of the Ministry of Agriculture resources in these selected weredas. The idea was first proposed by the Ministry of Agriculture and the World Bank in the early 1980s under the Peasant Agricultural Development Extension Program (PADEP) and was to include only the grain surplus awrajas in the Shewa, Arsi, and Gojam regions. The awrajas selected as "surplus-producing" under PADEP had relatively fertile land and stable weather conditions which are fundamental to the rain-dependent Ethiopian agriculture. The major objectives of PADEP were: (1) to increase the productivity of small holdings in these surplus-producing awrajas, which could then be distributed to other deficit areas; (2) the reform of the government-dominated marketing structure, which provided very low prices for farmers and restricted private traders and free movement of grain in the country; (3) the formation of an independent cooperative union that would represent the interest of farmers; (4) the decentralization of the Ministry of Agriculture's planning, financing, and extension activities; (5) the design and implementation of projects that would reflect the regions' agroecological and socioeconomic conditions; and (6) the deployment of extension agents at the district level and service cooperative level to promote local accountability.[20] The idea of PADEP was also supported by the Swedish International Development Authority, which participated in some of the negotiations.

Although the Ministry of Agriculture officials were sympathetic to PADEP, the Ethiopian government was suspicious and reluctant to give its support. This was partly due to fear that the organization would somehow undermine or conflict with the socialist programs the government had outlined. There was still no official agreement between the World Bank and the Ethiopian government on the major points of PADEP. However, since the 1984 famine, the Ethiopian government cleverly selected part of the package that it saw as having no conflict with its interests, and proceeded in implementing its own PADEP, partly to dispel the international image of a government whose agricultural policy was a major contributor to famine.

In 1985, the Ethiopian government proclaimed its priority for the attainment of food self-sufficiency. Some of the major ideas of PADEP, such as concentrating resources in "surplus-producing awrajas," became a national policy of "surplus-producing weredas," but with two modifications. The first modification was to limit the size of the operation to smaller, more manageable units at the wereda level instead of the awraja level—an improvement on the previous PADEP idea. The only irony is that the newly passed administrative structure of Ethiopia eliminated the wereda as an administrative unit. The second

Table 4.3 Number of Extension Agents in Each Awraja of Surplus-Producing Weredas

Awraja	Wereda	Number of Extension Agents
Borena	Debersina[a]	29
	Kelala	1
	Sayent	0
Wereilu	Wereilu[a]	12
	Jamma	14
	Leghida	5
Yeju	Habru[a]	20
	Gubalafto	7
Raya & Kobo	Kobo[a]	18
	Alamata	6

Source: Ministry of Agriculture Zonal Office in Dessie, Wollo
[a] Indicates surplus-producing wereda

modification involved expanding this policy into every region of Ethiopia, including the Wollo, Tigraye, and Eritrea regions frequently affected by famine. The findings from Wollo reveal that this change was most inappropriate there as the amount and distribution of rainfall is too unpredictable in these regions to invest in technical packages that rely heavily on adequate rainfall for food production. The great variability in rainfall pattern in Kobo (see Table 4.2) which is one of surplus-producing weredas, serves as a good example of the severe limitation of this approach.

In Wollo, the surplus-producing weredas included Debersina in Borena Awraja, Wereilu and Jamma in Wereilu Awraja, Habru in Yeju Awraja, Kobo and Alamata in Raya & Kobo Awraja (see Table 4.3). With the exception of Alamata, the sample in this study comprises all of the above weredas identified as surplus-producing. What essentially distinguished surplus-producing weredas from others in Wollo was the large number of extension agents assigned and the large quantity of fertilizer, improved seeds, pesticides, and other inputs allocated to these weredas. Prior to this policy, the number of extension agents was distributed fairly between the awrajas and the weredas. However, since this policy was introduced, serious imbalances resulted in the number of extension agents both among awrajas and between weredas in the same awraja (see Table 4.3).

It was shocking to find that every one of the so-called "surplus-producing weredas" (except Debersina), which had the most extension agents, were more severely affected by the 1987 drought than the nonsurplus-producing weredas. Even the uncharacteristic plain of Jamma, which was least affected by the 1984 famine, was given the highest priority for relief efforts in 1987. In fact, farmers in two of the selected peasant associations in this wereda were receiving food aid. On the other hand, Gubalafto Wereda (Yeju Awraja), not selected as a surplus-producing wereda, replaced Jamma Wereda in receiving the government's Agricultural Marketing Corporation award for meeting its quota and for providing the highest amount of grain in 1987. These findings suggest that the investment of resources in so-called surplus-producing weredas in a region like Wollo, where there is an even chance of having either a drought or a normal year, may have been unjustified.

Another important issue concerns the activities of the extension agents in these weredas, particularly during drought years. The major tasks of extension agents in these weredas were the provision of inputs, such as fertilizer, and the dissemination of advice on agricultural practices. In a drought year, neither fertilizer nor advice has any benefit. Even in normal years, the dissemination of information regarding fertilizer and improved seed during the dry season, when there is little farming activity is largely irrelevant. Needless to say, some extension agents in Kobo and Jamma candidly admitted having little work to do when this study was being conducted in what was considered a famine year in these weredas.

Conceptually, the idea of "surplus-producing weredas," which attempts to bring dramatic increase in food production quickly, may be appealing, but the way it is implemented seems to be detrimental to the long-term objective of attaining sustained food self-sufficiency in famine affected areas. The extension agents concentrated in the surplus-producing weredas were snatched from other weredas and awrajas where there was an urgent need to arrest land degradation. In Sayent Wereda (Borena Awraja), for instance, farmland is being turned to wasteland by severe erosion. Here the two tributaries of the Nile take massive topsoil from the highlands. No wereda deserved more extension agents to assist in reforestation and conservation efforts than Sayent. Yet, all of the extension agents working there were transferred to Debersina, the wereda least affected by the problem of land degradation.

The calamitous consequence of land degradation is evident in every highland of Wollo. As degradation destroys productive lands, more marginal lands are brought under cultivation. This process leads to an endless spiral that has brought most parts of this region to the brink of ecological collapse. The priority of any government program should be to take the swiftest possible action to arrest this vicious spiral. Instead, the awrajas (such as Lasta, Wag, Wadela Delanta, and Werehiminu) that face these grim prospects lost most or all of their extension agents, who were put to distributing fertilizer in the surplus-producing weredas. The Ministry of Agriculture's policy of concentrating efforts to create a surplus in a few weredas was plausible in other regions, but impractical in Wollo.

The diagnosis of famine in the Wollo region simply does not allow for any simplistic prescription, despite what the architects of the "surplus-producing wereda" lead us to believe. That fact is that fertilizer is not a cheap item for the Ethiopian government to import or for the peasants of Wollo to buy. Moreover, no amount of fertilizer can replace the amount of land that is being lost by degradation. In the absence of rain, accumulated fertilizer in Jamma, Habru, and Kobo weredas became the problem rather than the solution, taking up storage space that could be used for relief food. Yet, the success of "surplus-producing weredas" was calculated by the amount of fertilizer distributed to them. For example, a special report focusing only on the activities of surplus-producing weredas in Wollo highlighted that the average amount of fertilizer distributed in the surplus-producing weredas between 1980 and 1986 was 2,425 quintals, whereas in 1987 alone this figure swelled to 16,589 quintals.[21] It should be noted, however, that the fertilizer that was being distributed in Wollo was mostly donated by the various relief agencies working in Wollo. The Ministry of Agriculture could neither claim to be its source nor count on such aid for long. Furthermore, due to the absence of rain in many of the surplus-producing weredas in 1987, many farmers were not able to use the fertilizer that was distributed.

The solution to bringing an end to the human tragedy in Wollo should begin with measures that would arrest the cycle of ecological degradation and vulnerability to famine. The Ethiopian government's policy of concentrating resources in the "surplus-producing weredas" has little to contribute in ameliorating this problem. Moving around extension agents will not solve the problem of land degradation, which affects food production. Hence, the government response in dealing with famine is largely inappropriate in famine-prone regions such as Wollo.

Notes

1. Richard Pankhurst, "The History of Famine and Pestilence in Ethiopia Prior to the founding of Gonder," *Journal of Ethiopian Studies*, Volume 10, No. 2, Addis Ababa, 1972.

2. Mesfin Wolde-Mariam, *Rural Vulnerability to Famine in Ethiopia: 1958-77*, New Delhi: Vikas Publishing, 1984.

3. *Ibid.*, pp. 32-51.

4. Dawit Wolde Giorgis, *Red Tears: War, Famine and Revolution in Ethiopia*, Trenton, New Jersey: The Red Sea Press, 1989. See also: Kurt Jansson, Michael Harris, and Angela Penrose, *The Ethiopian Famine*, London: Zed Books Ltd., 1987.

5. Wolde-Mariam, *Rural Vulnerability*.

6. James McCann, "The Social Impact of Drought in Ethiopia: Oxen, Households, and Some Implications for Rehabilitation," in Michael Glantz, *Drought and Hunger in Africa: Denying Famine a Future*, Cambridge: Cambridge University Press, 1987.

7. Amartya Sen, *Poverty and Famine: An Essay on Entitlement and Deprivation*, Oxford: Oxford University Press, 1981. See also: Peter Cutler, "Famine Forecasting: Prices and Peasant Behavior in Northern Ethiopia," *Disaster*, Vol. 8, No. 1, 1984, pp. 48-55.

8. Data obtained from the Ministry of Agriculture Zonal Office at Dessie, Livestock

Development Department, Dessie, Wollo, December 1987.

9. McCann, "The Social Impact of Drought in Ethiopia," pp. 245-265.

10. Data generated from the Ministry of Agriculture North Eastern Zonal Office in Dessie, Wollo, January, 1989.

11. Of the four peasant associations selected in Wereilu Awraja, three were close to a river that could be tapped for irrigation. Both the peasant associations selected in the highland areas of Wereilu Wereda, Adama (017) and Batel (019), were close to a tributary of the Beto River, one of the two major tributaries of the Nile, originating from Wereilu Wereda. The other major tributary of the Nile is the Wayet River, which is in Jamma Wereda and is close to the Godo peasant association (024). Similarly, in Delanta Wereda (Wadela Delanta Awraja), the Goshmeda (03) peasant association is not too far from the Beshilo River, another major tributary of the Nile. In Borena Awraja (in both Debersina and Kelala weredas), the peasant associations selected have streams that are tributaries of the Yeshum River, a major tributary of the Nile.

12. P. K. R. Nair and E. Fernandes, *Agroforestry as an Alternative to Shifting Cultivation*, Nairobi: ICRAF Reprint No. 17, 1985, p. 2.

13. Dessalegn Rahmato, *Famine and Survival Strategies: A Case Study from Northeast Ethiopia*, Addis Ababa: Addis Ababa University, Institute of Development Research, May 1987, p. 3.

14. Rahmato, *Famine and Survival Strategies*.

15. Mesfin Wolde-Mariam, "Dimensions of Vulnerability to Famine," Paper presented at the National Conference on Disaster Prevention and Preparedness Strategy for Ethiopia, 5-8 December, Addis Ababa, p. 20.

16. The rainfall data on Table 3.3 for the most part is generated by the Institute of Agricultural Research and was later submitted to the National Meteorological Service. In cases when the data collected by the National Meteorological Service was incomplete, data from the Ministry of Agriculture, which also has a station in Kobo, were used. The verification of the rainfall data collected by the Institute of Agricultural Research and the Ministry of Agriculture in Kobo were similar but not identical in most cases.

17. Data obtained from the Ministry of Agriculture Office in Borena Awraja, Debersina Wereda, town of Mekanselam, Wollo, December 1987.

18. Data generated from the Ministry of Agriculture Zonal Office, Dessie, Wollo, December, 1987.

19. Eshetu Chole, "The Impact of War on the Ethiopian Economy," Paper presented to the Fourth Annual Conference on the Horn of Africa, City College of the City University of New York, May 26-28, 1989.

20. *Ethiopia: Reviews of Farmers' Incentives and Agricultural Marketing and Distribution Efficiency*, The World Bank, Washington D.C., 1983.

21. Ministry of Agriculture North Eastern Zonal Office, *A Report on the Activities of Surplus Producing Weredas*, written in Amharic, Dessie, Wollo, December 1988, p. 6.

5

Resettlement Reconsidered: Toward Self-Sufficiency or Disaster?

The sporadic movement of people from the northern regions to the central and southern regions of Ethiopia dates back at least to the seventeenth century. Such population movement became more common during the period of Ethiopia's expansion under Emperor Minilik, 1855 to 1913. In this century, particularly under Emperor Haile Selassie's rule, these spontaneous migrations became widespread and steady. This is partly due to the overall modernization effort of the country, which has resulted in the expansion of trade and communication, and partly due to population growth, shortage of land, and successive droughts in the northern highlands. Figures are difficult to cite, but millions of people voluntarily resettled between 1940 and 1970.[1] There was little government involvement in these activities; all of this movement took place quietly and smoothly, without the label of resettlement.

The planned resettlement of large numbers of people began after the 1973/74 Wollo famine, which claimed the lives of 200,000 people and was the worst famine in this century until 1984/85.[2] When the new military government (known as the *derg*) came to power in 1974, it bitterly condemned the imperial government's handling of the 1973/74 famine, only to be faced immediately with the problem of how to deal with the still lingering famine and its victims. The military government established the Relief and Rehabilitation Commission (RRC) as a means to deal with the recurrent famine in the north and to coordinate relief and rehabilitation projects in a systematic way. During the first ten years, 45,849 families (most of them from the drought-afflicted areas of the Wollo and Tigraye regions) were resettled in various regions of Ethiopia under the auspices of RRC.[3]

The highly publicized 1984 famine put enormous pressure on the Ethiopian government, which was accused of spending millions of dollars on the celebration of the tenth anniversary of the socialist revolution while famine was raging in the north. At the height of the 1984/85 famine, eight million people were affected by drought in Ethiopia. The worst hit regions were Wollo and Tigraye. In Wollo, 2.6 million people were affected from the total population of 3.6 million; and in Tigraye, 1.4 million people were affected from the population of 2.4 million.[4]

Faced with such a magnitude of famine victims and mounting international criticism of its agricultural policy, the Ethiopian government opted for a quick fix and chose resettlement as the most viable option to deal with this problem. Referring to the victims as "environmental refugees," the Ethiopian government announced an "emergency resettlement" program to resettle 1.5 million people from the famine-affected areas, particularly from Wollo and Tigraye, within a year.[5] Indeed, from November 1984 until March 1986, 594,190 family members were resettled in the Illubabor, Wellega, Keffa, Gojam and Gonder regions.[6] The largest number of the settlers, 374,432, came from the Wollo region; the second largest (107,230) from the Shewa region; the third (89,716) from the Tigraye region.[7] The majority of the settlers (81%) went to the southwestern regions of Wellega, Illubabor, and Keffa. Most of the remaining (17%) went to the Italian-assisted resettlement scheme in Metekel (Gojam region), while about 2% settled in the Gonder region.[8]

The government action to resettle so many people may be dramatic, but the rationale for the resettlement on environmental grounds is supported by the Ethiopian Highland Reclamation Study, financed by the United Nations Food and Agricultural Organization. The Ethiopian highlands suffer from massive land degradation due to soil erosion. If this degradation continues, 18% of the highland will be bare rock by the year 2010 and 10 million people will not be able to produce food from the land.[9] This severe degradation is largely caused by the enormous pressure exerted on the ecosystem by human activity, including intensive cultivation, overgrazing, overpopulation, and deforestation. In particular, the objective of the resettlement program was to restore the loss of productive land affected by drought and to use the vast amount of land in the fertile southwestern region to increase food production and generate rural income.

The criteria for selecting the weredas and peasant associations for resettlement were: topography of rugged hills and slopes exceeding 35%; severe deforestation and/or severe erosion; few natural resources and poor soil; affliction by recurrent famine in the past 25 years; and population density to the point where average land size is too small to sustain a family.[10]

The magnitude of land degradation is visible in many parts of the highlands of Wollo. During the fieldwork it was evident that a number of peasant associations had a slope exceeding 30%, high population and livestock density and little vegetative cover. The data from peasant associations presented in Table 3.2 serve as examples of the severity of degradation in Wollo. These peasant associations are characterized by numerous and expanding gullies, large human and livestock density, and diminishing land size for both cropping and grazing. The carrying capacity of the land is either surpassed or seriously threatened. In principle, there are legitimate grounds for relocating farmers from these highly degraded areas to areas where these farmers could be self-sufficient. In reality, however, the experience of the resettlement program in dealing with degradation has been futile.

This study will focus on assessing peasants' perceptions towards resettlement, its environmental impact in Wollo and in settlement areas in southwestern Ethiopia, and its contribution in making settlers self-sufficient in food. Wollo serves as an ideal case study in examining these issues since the government resettlement program concentrated on Wollo and the majority of the settlers come from Wollo.

Peasants' Views on Resettlement

Many journalistic accounts of the 1984 "emergency resettlement" portrayed it as a program enforced by wholesale terrorizing of the famine victims. Others perceived resettlement as a plot by an Amhare-dominated government to take Oromos land in the relatively fertile regions by moving the Christian highlanders (mainly Amhares and Tigre) from the famine-affected northern regions.[11] This is an example of outsiders' superficial understanding of Ethiopian politics, which is, by and large, inscrutable even to Ethiopians who closely follow political events in Ethiopia. Such an extreme view most probably serves to undermine the genuine opposition of many Ethiopian officials and scholars to resettlement rather than to influence the Ethiopian government. This view also misses the fundamental rationale behind resettlement, which is initiated and supported by several of the United Nations agencies (mainly the Food and Agricultural Organization) and some Western countries.

The 1984/85 resettlement in Wollo was not entirely undertaken by brute force. At the same time, peasant departure was far from joyful. Most peasants left voluntarily, seeking, under the circumstances, the only available alternative for survival. Certainly, there have been abuses, with incidents of people abducted while en route to the market, to church, or to peasant association meetings. High level officials, on occasion, have intervened to put an end to such practices. Nearly all of the peasants interviewed in this study vigorously expressed that they did not wish to be resettled. Peasants' attitudes toward resettlement was decisively negative everywhere in Wollo. Why did peasants' attitudes toward resettlement dramatically shift from acceptance in 1984 to defiance in 1987?

First, the 1984 resettlement began badly. Wollo was in a state of chaos due primarily to the massive number of people pouring into relief centers. Because of crowded conditions, not all members of families were admitted. There were cases in which some of the family were staying in relief centers while other members were receiving food assistance while still on the farm or in the nearby town. The majority of those who were in relief centers left for resettlement. In the process of traveling to resettlement areas, members of the same families sometimes left by different buses and were sent to different destinations, resulting in separation.

Second, about half of the interviewed farmers knew someone who had escaped from a resettlement area. Those who returned told of their frightening experiences to those who were about to be recruited. Peasants naturally trusted the first-hand information they received from their fellow peasants and relatives rather than what they were told by local party officials. Third, like a wedding, mourning also has an elaborate ceremony within every rural community in Ethiopia. During the fieldwork, we were witnesses when peasants and their community mourned the death of a relative in a resettlement area.

Fourth, peasants are deeply attached to their community and have an unwavering loyalty to their birthplace. A familiar response for not wanting to resettle was that "they would rather die in a place where their umbilical cord is buried." A corollary to this was the feeling of many peasants, expressed by one of the interviewed farmers in the Gobeya peasant association (012), Tehulederie Wereda (Ambassel Awraja), who responded to the question of why he would not like to be resettled by asking me why he should risk moving his family to a place where they might not be able to adjust. Finally, many felt that they would be able to grow enough food for their families during normal years and saw no need to resettle elsewhere.

Like the famine itself, the 1984 resettlement left scars on nearly every village of Wollo. Of the interviewed farmers, 85% reported knowing someone in their community who had left for resettlement. A number acknowledged that their own relatives had resettled. However, for a significant number of peasants who left for resettlement, their final destination was Wollo. In this sample, 48% of the respondents knew someone who had returned to Wollo after resettlement. The government agencies in Wollo, although secretive about this, acknowledged that 15,047 formerly resettled peasants returned due to favorable weather conditions in Wollo.[12] In our estimation, the real figure was likely to be at least three to five times higher than that.

When this author returned to the settlement areas in the Illubabor and Keffa regions in January and February 1989, the number of those who had abandoned the settlement areas was reported to have substantially increased. No figure was cited. This surprised party officials and some of the Ministry of Agriculture staff who believed that the number would dwindle as settlers adjusted to the new conditions. The news of the bumper harvest in Wollo in 1988 may have stirred the Wollo settlers to return; but it is unlikely to be the only reason for the very high number of returnees.

It was difficult to obtain the exact figure on the number of returnees in Wollo. Returnees lived as fugitives, fearful of being caught and sent back; they were not entitled to land in a peasant association. One of the few places where these returnees actually identified themselves and informed us about their plight was in the Kelo peasant association (02), located 5 kilometers from the town of Kemissie in Kalu Awraja. In this peasant association, sixty-eight heads of household left for resettlement in 1984/85, thirty of whom had returned. Reasons for their return included health problems, the death of a family member, poor working conditions and harvests on huge farms, a desire to reunite with family members, hostility among natives, and homesickness.

The government plan called for resettling 50,000 heads of household (209,000 family members) in one year's time beginning in October 1987.[13] The problem with this plan was that, like most plans in Ethiopia, it was exceedingly ambitious. It was also ridden by internal contradictions in its guidelines. On the one hand, the guidelines stated that recruitment for resettlement was to be pursued on an entirely voluntary basis. On the other hand, quotas were assigned to each wereda on the number of families that must resettle.

These guidelines became a puzzle to everyone, including some Ministry of Agriculture officials at the wereda level. On the eve of our interview, in the Ashinga peasant association (01) in Sayent Wereda, Borena Awraja, local officials and peasant association leaders rounded up forty heads of household along with their family members for resettlement. They were sent to Dessie (the capital city of Wollo), only to be sent back to their homes after they informed officials there that they were forced to leave their homes. In discussing this incident with party officials and administrators in the Relief and Rehabilitation Commission in Dessie, their tendency was to blame some zealous local administrators. While there is some truth to this, the justification that has led to such abuses is the resettlement quota. There should have been no need for quotas if the government was serious in its declaration that resettlement was to be voluntary.

To set quotas for resettlement may have been easy, but to enforce them proved futile. As of March 1988, voluntary resettlement yielded about 1,785 family members, all of them coming from relief centers.[14] In their attempt to recruit peasants for resettlement, peasant association leaders and extension agents were even attacked. The government, at least for the moment, wisely abandoned obligatory quotas for resettlement in Wollo and shifted pressure to the Ministry of Agriculture's staff and extension agents, who were accused of failing to give a more convincing sermon on the virtues of resettlement to a peasantry that did not know its own interest. Perhaps the fine line between voluntary and coerced resettlement is captured by the notion of "bego teseno," to which party officials and political cadres carefully and skillfully reverted when voluntariness fails. "Bego" means goodness or kindness, and "teseno" means coercion. Hence, "bego teseno" literally means coercion for someone's own good. This is to say, for those who do not know their own interest, coercion is a legitimate means of helping them realize it. This is similar to what Marx called "false consciousness."

The question is: can resettlement arrest degradation and restore ecological balance in Wollo? Resettlement temporarily reduces the amount of human pressure exerted on the land. However, it does not control the increasing population that contributes to land pressure. At the present rate of over 2.9% population growth, Ethiopia's population will be three times greater (114.5 million) by the year 2015.[15] Neither does it prevent the return of people to the area. The Jerjero peasant association (014), for example, in Kutaber Wereda, Dessie Zurie Awarja, meets all the criteria for resettlement. This peasant association was devastated by the 1984 famine; some peasants abandoned their farming, a few died, and most (about 300 families) left for resettlement. Shortly after the resettlement, about 160 members were reported in this peasant association. At the time of this study there were 268 members, with an increase of over 100 members within the last three years. What caused this increase is somewhat of a puzzle. It is likely that the cause was an influx from nearby peasant associations in an effort to claim the abandoned land, rather than young members of the association who were independently registering as new members. At any rate, this limited observation suggests that resettlement can siphon off a segment of the population, but it cannot arrest its replenishment, which is essential to combating land degradation.

Among the major causes of land degradation are livestock density and grazing patterns. The resettlement program focuses only on humans and does little to address the role of livestock in the process of land degradation. In fact, those who are exempted from resettlement often have many livestock (particularly oxen), which are an indicator of being self-supporting. Resettlement also created a great deal of uncertainty and insecurity among the peasants in Wollo. Thus, peasants were not motivated to undertake conservation activities, fearing that they might be forced to resettle at any time. This was evident in our observation that individual initiative in planting trees was negligible, and most of tree planting was being carried out collectively in community forests. In addition, as indicated in Table 2.8, farmers were not planting trees because they feared that they would be confiscated by the peasant association, or because they feared resettlement. Extension agents and peasant association leaders who were promoting conservation and afforestation activities publicly admitted that the unease over resettlement had constrained peasant participation in such efforts. Hence, the objective of halting environmental degradation via resettlement was having the opposite effect.

Peasants' Conditions in Settlement Areas

The western part of Ethiopia has an area of 175,300 square kilometers, of which the Wellega region covers 41%, the Illubabor 31%, and the Keffa 28% of the total area. This is one of the most sparsely populated regions of the country, containing 6.5 million people. The dominant ecological zones are a medium altitude zone covering 46% of the area (1,500 to 2,500 meters above sea level), and a lowland zone covering 45% of the area (500 to 1,500 meters). Only 4% of the area is considered to be arid land and is less than 500 meters above sea level. It is estimated that half of Ethiopia's remaining natural forests are located in these regions (particularly in Illubabor).[16]

The peasants of Wollo made their new homes in one of three types of resettlement schemes: "large-scale," "low-cost," and "integrated" settlements. The most significant were "large-scale" settlements, where 224,576 people were settled, and "integrated" settlements (placement within existing peasant associations), where 252,442 settled. [17] Only 26,888 people settled under "low-cost" settlement schemes. [18]

The large-scale settlement scheme was hastily prepared under the 1984 emergency program by clearing large amounts of forest land in sparsely populated areas. Huge estates of 8,000 to 20,000 hectares of land, with 6,000 to 16,000 heads of household, were broken down into smaller units of 1,000 to 2,000 hectares and about 500 heads of household. These units were further divided into villages. This scheme is highly mechanized, involving many tractors and combines, similar to state farms or communes. The peasants are transformed overnight into daily workers on a modern farm with little understanding of the system. Agriculture is organized like the outdated communes that existed in China and the Soviet Union. The management collects all of the harvest and then distributes the products based on labor contribution. Peasants strongly disliked this collective system, which they felt was not rewarding to those who work hard. They candidly expressed that they worked more diligently on their small individual plots than on the collectives. The only individual land the peasants own under this scheme are small plots (considerably less than half a hectare) around their homesteads. Most of the "large-scale" settlements were located in lowland areas and on flat land. [19]

The difference between low-cost and large-scale settlements is one of magnitude. The low-cost settlement is usually established on the smaller estates of less than 1,000 hectares and has considerably fewer tractors and modern equipment. As with large settlement schemes, low-cost settlements are also run on cooperative principles. Members contribute their labor and receive the produce at the end of the year, based on a point system—a system that was deeply resented by peasants, irrespective of the scheme. There were nine "low-cost" schemes, all located in the Keffa region. [20]

Of these, the Kishe and the Miche settlements were established on a nationalized modern farm following the Agrarian Reform. The rest of the low-cost schemes were built by clearing dense forest area, in a manner similar to the large-scale settlements. In addition to being smaller and less mechanized, the low-cost settlements have more individual plots around the homesteads and the peasants are given oxen to plough them. Most peasants attributed the production of the bulk of their harvest to their individual plots, and not to the modern collectives.

In the integrated settlement, peasants are placed within existing peasant associations and are allocated land to farm individually. The selection of a peasant association, as well as the number of people who are located in one area, is based on the size of the peasant association and on the number of households therein. As of 1988, the number of heads of household under the integrated scheme in Illubabor was 89,849, in Wellega 59,947, and in Keffa 46,247. [21] A large part of these settlements were located in the fertile and densely forested highlands of Illubabor, which had a little more than one million inhabitants and 4.6 million hectares of land.[22] In this region, forest land is relatively plentiful. One Wollo peasant who had resettled said: "All we have to do is clear more forests if we need more land to cultivate."

Since the resettlement program was shunned by many donor agencies and Western countries, it has largely been financed by the Ethiopian government. The average annual cost for settlements from 1985 to 1988 is estimated at 58,075,000 Ethiopian birr ($29,037,750).[23] This does not include the manpower expense of the various ministries. Hence, it is a very expensive program given Ethiopia's resources. The cost incurred by this program, and whether it is self-sufficient, are fundamental issues in evaluating its success. However, the information on these issues is too limited to make a reliable assessment. Based on field observation and discussions with officials and extension agents intimately involved in the supervision of the settlements, it seemed certain that large-scale settlements incur the highest cost. One of the few studies done on this issue pointed out that the total cost incurred from the time a peasant leaves his previous farm until he is self-sufficient in his new setting is 2,338 birr per person for large-scale settlements, and 802 birr per person for low-cost settlements.[24] The cost of the integrated settlements is likely to be lower than even the low-cost scheme because the only major costs, transportation and feeding until the first harvest, do not involve farm machinery or input expenses. Another study has shown that low-cost settlements are more cost effective than large-scale settlements.[25]

The issue of self-sufficiency is a difficult, yet important, issue that needs to be addressed. A commonly employed way of comparing self-sufficiency is annual yield per hectare, but the kinds of crops grown and the amount of input used in each scheme are so vastly different that such a comparison would be unfair. Be that as it may, one of the few systematic studies on self-sufficiency pointed out that the average annual yield for a farmer on a large-scale settlement was 11 quintals per hectare; on a low-cost settlement, 5 quintals; and on an integrated settlement, 6 quintals.[26] The report went on to state that the relatively high yield on large-scale settlements did not mean self-sufficiency. Farming was done by tractors and state-employed workers. There was little market for the maize produced as these settlements were located in remote lowland areas. Hence, farmers had less purchasing power and lacked more household items and consumer goods than those in the integrated settlements. It was reported that only two large-scale settlements were relatively self-sufficient, while the rest depended on government support. A sixty-year-old settler from Kelala Wereda (Borena Awraja) in Wollo pointed out, "I have received more relief food here in the last three years than I had for so many years in Wollo." In the two settlement sites covered in this study, Ekuna Kijang and Baro Abol, the yields averaged 2 quintals/hectare for sorghum and 5 quintals/hectare for maize. Such low yields were obtained in spite of mechanization and the availability of fertilizer and improved seed.[27]

Low-cost settlements, also heavily dependent on government subsidies, suffered equally from lack of markets to sell their produce and from severe shortage of consumer goods. Some, like Chunege, Gale, and Gura Ferda, were totally dependent on food assistance, and the Ministry of Agriculture staff in Jima recommended that these settlement sites be moved elsewhere. In all, the low-cost and large-scale settlement programs have drastically fallen short of attaining food self-sufficiency and improving the peasants' productivity. The major impediment is lack of incentive to produce due to the collective-style farming and distribution.

Integrated settlements were by far the least dependent on government assistance. The low productivity of settlers in these schemes stemmed largely from a serious shortage of oxen and lack of input. Some of the settlers under this scheme, who settled around coffee growing areas in Keffa and Illubabor, became well-to-do farmers. In all, irrespective of productivity, those in integrated settlements tended to be more self-sufficient in food than those in the large-scale or low-cost settlements.

Perhaps the most significant consideration in assessing the relative success of resettlement schemes is finding out whether settlers feel at home in their new surroundings. In this regard the highest rating went to integrated settlements and the lowest to large-scale settlements. Unquestionably, the integrated settlement was the most humane and appropriate scheme, functioning with little social disorder. Under this scheme, peasants owned their own land, kept bee hives in their back yards, and above all were in control of the fruits of their labor. In sum, peasant farmers lived under similar conditions as they did in Wollo, a fact not well understood or appreciated by high-level policymakers. Even the climate, mostly in the medium altitude zones, was more suitable to the Wollo settlers than the large-scale settlements, which were located in very hot lowland areas.

Peasants under integrated settlements did not report having as many chronic problems as those in the large-scale and low-cost settlements. Since coming to the settlement areas, fewer peasants in the integrated schemes reported the death or the serious illness of a family member. However, in the large-scale settlements, nearly every household interviewed, particularly in Gambela, mourned the loss of a family member and indicated facing serious health problems, such as malaria and elephantiasis.

The hostility one often heard about between settlers (mostly Amhares and Tigres) and natives (predominately Oromos) was exaggerated. One field study on settlement areas indicated a cordial relationship between the natives and settlers, which sometimes resulted in intermarriage when the settlers and natives shared the same religion.[28] Similarly, most of the Wollo settlers interviewed in the integrated settlements in Mocha, Gore, and Buno Bedela awrajas, in Illubabor, said the natives treated them fairly well. One of the interviewed settlers, who came from Delanta Wereda (Wadela Delanta Awraja) in Wollo, explained that he had no complaints against the natives but against the government, which put him in the middle of a forest with no church nearby (Wadela Delanta is one of the strongholds of Christianity in Wollo).

The natives also acknowledged that they learned a great deal about farming from the Wollo settlers. Most Wollo settlers were now experimenting with different cereals and crops such as wheat, peas, beans and lentils, and oil seeds; some were harvesting twice a year through *belg* cultivation, an unknown practice in the native agriculture. One aspect about which the natives and Wollo settlers seemed to be at odds was that the Wollo settlers, even in the integrated settlements, did not feel at home. They talked about Wollo constantly and displayed an unabashed love and loyalty for Wollo. The natives felt the settlers should be grateful to live in a region where rain was plentiful. Too much rain, however, was one of the Wollo settlers' complaints, because it limited them to growing maize and restricted them from growing the variety of cereals they grew in Wollo during normal years.

The large-scale settlement scheme was inappropriate for two reasons. First, they were located in hot lowland and semiarid regions, to which Wollo settlers found it difficult to adjust. Second, the settlers disliked the collective form of production and had little understanding about the highly mechanized large-scale scheme. Needless to say, many of the people who escaped were from the large-scale settlements. According to one report, of the 52,000 heads of household who were settled under the "emergency program," about 45,000 had escaped, and 7,000 had died. Among those in the integrated scheme, about 4,000 heads of household were reported to have escaped, while another 4,000 had died.[29] Most Wollo settlers we met in the large-scale resettlement scheme would have liked to return to Wollo; as one said: "I do not even believe I am in Ethiopia."

The Environmental Threat in Settlement Areas

Increasing agricultural production in Ethiopia will largely depend on good soil. Irrespective of the settlement scheme, resettlement has had an adverse impact on soil fertility. The indiscriminate clearing of forest with bulldozers and other heavy equipment, for both large-scale and low-cost settlements, has led to the removal of topsoil within 10 to 20 centimeters, a part of the soil which is crucial in maintaining fertility. Hans Hurni's study of integrated settlements in Il-lubabor reveals that, there, too, the incidence of erosion on cultivated plots after forest clearing was much more severe than the incidence of erosion on tradi-tional fields.[30] This is mainly because, on traditional fields, the native farmers kept perennial crops, such as false banana (amharic name *enset*) and coffee, and did most of their cultivation around their homesteads. Thus, the native farming system allowed for year-round woody vegetation and grass cover that protected the soil from erosion. In addition, there were many integrated settlements in relatively hilly areas. Settlers as well as natives were cultivating the slopes without terraces or soil bunds. Contour ploughing was not widely practiced. Such practices, along with the massive deforestation (triggered by resettlement), will result in topsoil erosion in the highlands of Illubabor.

The native farming system is a hoe culture that depends on propagating root crops, particularly *enset*, as opposed to the grain plough agriculture practiced by the settlers.[31] The natives plant their staple (*Enset ventricosum*) once every five to ten years and supplement it by cultivating maize, their main crop, each year. Maize is usually planted around their homesteads and hardly requires the clearing of large areas of forest land. Although there was no crop rotation practiced by the natives, their farming practice had a minimal adverse impact on soil fertility. However, settlers who practiced crop rotation in Wollo did not practice it in the settlement area. A major reason for this was food habit. The settlers from Wollo and Tigraye strongly disliked *enset* and were having a hard time adjusting to eating maize, which had become their major crop. They used maize to make *enjera* instead of teff (the Ethiopian staple food). The Wollo settlers made numerous attempts to grow teff but it got waterlogged in most areas. In addition, there was little attempt on the part of the Ministry of Agriculture to introduce different kinds of cereals in settlements areas. Crop rotation becomes essential in maintaining soil fertility as an increasing amount of land is brought into cultivation each year in settlement areas.

The clearing of forest has also become widespread in integrated settlements. Shifting cultivation has expanded, and there is a growing demand to meet the basic necessities of the settlers in the construction and provision of houses, fuelwood, and farming equipment. The burning of forest, a common practice among the natives, is more detrimental now because the fallow years will be reduced due to the increasing demand for land for cultivation. Moreover, the settlers seemed to be overwhelmed by the dense forest around them and often complained of wildlife destroying their crops and threatening their families. Hence, they readily cut trees without much thought about its effect.

Perhaps the most notable change observed during the second fieldwork in January 1989 was that settlers were using wood and wood products as a source of cash. Since the construction of roads leading to nearby towns, settlers who lived close to the roads were selling charcoal, the making of which has been the means whereby trees around the major towns in Ethiopia, such as Addis Ababa, have been destroyed. Settlers were making chairs, tables, and other household items not only for their own use, but also to sell. In fact, the sites of integrated settlements were easily distinguishable in Mocha Awraja: they occupied open fields with little woody vegetation in the midst of thick forest.

In all, these findings clearly suggest that resettlement poses an enormous environmental threat. No one has articulated this threat more than the committee appointed by the Council of Ministers to investigate the condition of resettlement in the western region of Ethiopia. The committee, headed by Ato Aklu

Environment, Famine, and Politics in Ethiopia

Clearing of rainforest for agriculture and settlement, Mocha, Illubabor.

The wanton cutting of trees around a homestead in a settlement area, Gore, Illubabor.

Girgire, the former vice minister of the Natural Resource Department of the Ministry of Agriculture, gave one of the most candid appraisals of the existing conditions. The committee's findings emphasized that unless concerted efforts were taken to arrest the accelerating rate of deforestation and soil erosion, there would be a major imbalance in the ecosystem in the settlement areas within eight years. The magnitude of this imbalance and degradation would be similar to that of the famine-affected areas of the northern highlands of Ethiopia.[32] The committee's assessment reflects the sober realities of the massive degradation that was taking place in most of the settlement areas. The findings of this study provide further evidence to substantiate those of the committee.

Party officials (members of the politburo) often intervened in the selection of settlement sites with little regard for the advice of the Ministry of Agriculture officials and field staff, whose commitment to the resettlement program was considered dubious. Perhaps one of the greatest contributors to environmental degradation, irrespective of the kind of settlement scheme, was the absence of systematic land use planning in the selection of sites. The measures of land quality that were used by the Ministry of Agriculture Land Use and Regulatory Department were ignored in the implementation of resettlement programs. These indicators are temperature regime, growing period and moisture availability, drainage, degradation hazard, nutrient status and nutrient retention, rooting conditions, toxicities, land preparation requirements, the potential for mechanization and workability, and pests and diseases.[33]

An important measure of land suitability for cropping is soil drainage, that is, the availability of oxygen around the root zone. The drainage ability provides an adequate balance of air and water for crop growth. The soil in most of Gambela has a cement-like layer that hinders water absorption and is believed to be deficient in organic content. Excessive water limits air circulation and plants eventually perish. Under the "emergency" resettlement in 1985, the Ministry of Construction selected a settlement site in the Gilo valley in Gambela (mainly because it was close to the Gilo River) and cultivated 8,000 hectares of maize. No yields were obtained since water could not penetrate below 35 cm because of the hard layer underneath. The corn fields were drenched during the rainy season and by floods from the nearby Gilo River. Needless to say, this settlement site was abandoned a year later and settlers moved to another site in Abobo. Even the settlement areas that have good drainage, had surprisingly low yields, as extension agents secretly admit. They averaged about 4 to 5 quintals per hectare for maize and sorghum in spite of mechanization and the availability of fertilizer and improved seed.[34] The low-cost settlements in Dedesa (at Dedesa valley) and Miche in the Keffa region also suffered from poor water drainage, which adversely affected yields in those areas.

Settlement sites were also selected with total disregard for land preparation requirements and potential for mechanization. The low-cost settlement schemes at Gura Ferda and Gale were established on rugged terrain with steep slopes, which made cultivation difficult, especially using tractors. The soil depth in these sites, particularly at Gura Ferda, was shallow. This fact was acknowledged by the Ministry of Agricultural staff in Jima, which recommended to the local party officials that settlers at Gura Ferda and Gale should be resettled elsewhere. Since their establishment, neither settlement has produced enough food and their settlers were totally dependent on food assistance from the Relief and Rehabilitation Commission.

There was a serious shortage of land in most of the low-cost settlements. The average holding was 0.96 hectare and there seemed to be little possibility of expanding land in the Chunege, the Gale, and the Gura Ferda settlements.[35] Most of the settlers in the integrated settlements presently had adequate land. However, this situation could drastically change because of an influx of people into areas with limited capacity to expand in the fertile highland areas, and because of the high rate of population growth. A preliminary report on the large-scale settlement in Jaresso indicated a population growth rate as high as 4%.[36] Settlement sites in both the large-scale and low-cost schemes were also established where there were serious shortages of water (in Gambela and Miche), where wildlife was threatened (in Gambela and Milgawa), and where there was a devastating livestock disease known as "gendi" (in Gale and Chunege). Thus, the establishment of most of the settlement sites did not take into account the land potential needed to support the settlers for the long term.

Some field extension agents mentioned that some of the settlement sites were selected when party officials were travelling by helicopter. This is not an entirely sarcastic remark, but a story that has some truth. In fairness, Ministry of Agriculture officials and its staff at the field level were often in conflict with party officials concerning the establishment of sites under the "emergency resettlement" program. The differences between the two were such that the Ministry of Construction was given a clear mandate by party officials to establish both the large-scale and the low-cost settlements. There were several instances when there were open attacks on the Ministry of Agriculture Land Use Planning and Regulatory Department staff, who had become vocal in their opposition to the selection of some of the settlement sites.

The major obstacle in the resettlement program appeared to be that no single ministry was delegated the authority to run it, creating what Alula Pankhurst calls "the orphan child" of the government.[37] This has resulted in the intervention of party officials and others in the Ministry of Construction who have little understanding about agriculture. However, this is in no way to suggest the creation of another ministry for resettlement since the burgeoning of a centralized bureaucracy is the most serious impediment to undertaking development projects in Ethiopia. The Ministry of Agriculture is the most appropriate agency to have the authority for the resettlement program as it is the only ministry that has the technical and the manpower capacity for such a complex task.

When all is said and done, the most important consideration for the Ethiopian government is not to promote resettlement, but rather to reduce the need for it. The single-minded effort of the resettlement program to remove humans will be insignificant in averting the massive land degradation found in the famine-affected regions such as Wollo. Removing humans does not control population growth rates. The resettlement program ignores the role of livestock in the process of land degradation. Fear of resettlement had created uncertainty among farmers, inadvertently undermining rehabilitation and afforestation efforts in Wollo.

There are some legitimate cases for resettlement if it is implemented with careful planning and on a voluntary basis. Resettlement should be an option available to anyone who would like to settle anywhere at any time. Resettlement based on the principle of voluntariness would require a decentralized approach, which would delegate more authority to peasant associations and local Ministry of Agriculture offices and less to party officials. Once again, the issue of the participation of the peasantry figures prominently.

The findings from this study emphasize that the resettlement program presents an ominous environmental threat in settlement areas and has not resulted in attaining food self-sufficiency among settlers. Hence, the belief that a highly centralized and subsidized resettlement program is to be a source of prosperity for Ethiopia remains a myth. For a future without famine in Ethiopia, the most crucial effort is to take measures that will arrest the root causes that have lead to resettlement. This would mean giving the highest priorities to conservation and rehabilitation efforts in Wollo and other highly degraded regions of the Ethiopian highlands.

Notes

1. Adrian P. Wood, "Resettlement in Illubabor Province, Ethiopia," (Ph.D Thesis, University of Liverpool, England, October 1977), p. 84.

2. The Relief and Rehabilitation Commission, *The Challenges of Drought: Ethiopia's Decade of Struggle in Relief and Rehabilitation*, Addis Ababa, 1985, p. 19.

3. J. Colaris Samuel with Yibrah Hagos, *Resettlement Strategy Proposals*, Ethiopian Highland Reclamation Study, Addis Ababa, 1985, p. 16.

4. Kurt Jansson, Michael Harris, and Angela Penross, *The Ethiopian Famine*, New Jersey: Zed Books Ltd., p. xii.

5. Samuel, *Resettlement Strategy Proposals*, p. 50.

6. Data obtained from an official chart at the Relief and Rehabilitation Commission in Addis Ababa, March 1988.

7. *Resettlement Activities from the Sending Regions*, Document written in Amharic, Council of Ministers (PDRE), Host Region Study Committee, Addis Ababa, March, 1988. Also *The Ethiopian Herald*, March 9, 1988, reported that 360,000 families had been resettled from Wollo since 1984.

8. Data obtained from an official chart at the Relief and Rehabilitation Commission in Addis Ababa, March 1988.

9. M. Constable and Members of the Ethiopian Highland Reclamation Study, *The Degradation of Resources and an Evaluation of Actions to Combat It*, Working Paper 19, Ministry of Agriculture, Addis Ababa, December 1984, pp. 29- 48.

10. Regional Planning Office for North Eastern Ethiopia, *A Special Planning Document Prepared to Deal with the 1987 Drought in Wollo*, Document Written in Ahmaric, Dessie, Wollo, October 1987, pp. 63- 64.

11. Jason W. Clay and Bonnie K. Holcomb, *Politics and the Ethiopian Famine, 1984-1985*, Cultural Survival Report 20, 1986, pp. 165-176.

12. Regional Planning Office for North Eastern Ethiopia, *A Special Planning Document Prepared to Deal With the 1987 Drought in Wollo*, p. 14.

13. Ibid., p. 21. This quota was not set in Wollo but with the approval of the highest government and party officials in Addis Ababa.

14. *The Ethiopian Herald*, Wednesday March 9, 1989, p. 1.

15. Central Statistics Authority, *Population Projection of Ethiopia: Total and Sectoral*, Population Studies Series No. 2, Addis Ababa, March 1988, p. 29.

16. Regional Planning Office for Western Ethiopia, *A Study of Resettlement Activities: 1985-1988*, Document written in Amharic, Jima, August 1988, pp. 4-6.

17. Ibid., p. 8.

18. Ministry of Agriculture Zonal Office for Western Ethiopia, *A Study of Low-Cost Settlement Schemes in Keffa*. Document written in Amharic, Jima, January 1988, p. 26.

19. Regional Planning Office for Western Ethiopia, *A Study of Resettlement Activities*, pp. 11 and 42.

All the "large-scale" settlement schemes were in Wellega (Asosa, Keto, Jareso, Anger Guten), with the exception of one in Illubabor at Gambela. The largest one of these schemes was Asosa which had 14,143 heads of household (47,079 family members) and 18,808 hectares of land. Gambela was the second largest with 11,234 heads of household (44,664 family members) and 15,600 hectares of land. Keto had 10,397 heads of household (37,024 family members) and 11,234 hectares; Anger Guten had 9,756 heads of household (29,217 family members) and 12,329 hectares; and Jareso had 3,860 heads of household (13,528 family members) and 4,644 hectares of land.

20. Ministry of Agriculture Zonal Office for Western Ethiopia, *A Study of Low Cost Resettlement*, pp. 26-43.

These were the Gura Ferda with 4,121 heads of household and 2,323 hectares; the Milgawa with 344 heads of household and 304 hectares; the Arguba with 554 heads of household and 477 hectares; the Kishe with 891 heads of household and 883 hectares; the Miche with 666 heads of household and 1,053 hectares; the Dedesa with 292 heads of household and 512 hectares; the Begi with 502 heads of household and 620 hectares; the Chunege with 570 heads of household and 481 hectares; and the Gale with 378 heads of household and 354 hectares of land.

21. Regional Planning Office for Western Ethiopia, *A Study of Resettlement Activities*, p. 10.

22. Central Statistical Authority, *Area by Region, Awraja, Wereda*, Addis Ababa: Statistical Bulletin 49, 1986, p. 30.

23. Eshetu Chole and Teshome Mulat, "Land Settlement in Ethiopia: A Review of Developments," in A. S. Oberai, *Land Settlement Policies and Population Redistribution in Developing Countries: Achievements, Problems and Prospects*, New York: Praeger, 1988, p. 198.

24. Samuel, *Resettlement Strategy Proposals*, p. 44.

25. Chole and Mulat, "Land Settlement in Ethiopia," pp. 178-182.

26. *Resettlement in Post-Revolutionary Ethiopia: Results, Problems, and Future Prospects*, Document written in Amharic, Council of Ministers (PDRE), Host Region Study Committee, Main Report. Addis Ababa, 1988.

27. Data obtained in Ekuna Kijang and Baro Abol settlement villages in Gambela. These figures are also cited by unofficial report written by the Ministry of Agriculture Office, Metu, Illubabor.

28. Alula Pankhurst, "Resettlement in Ethiopia: Orphan Child of Herald of Change," Paper presented at Conference on Options in Rural Development, Bergen, Norway, July 1989.

29. *Resettlement in Post-Revolutionary Ethiopia*.

30. This information was obtained from discussion and correspondence with Professor Hans Hurni regarding the question as to which settlement schemes pose serious environmental threat.

31. Details on the hoe and plough culture is presented in E. Westphal, *Pluses in Ethiopia, Their Taxonomy and Agricultural Significance*, The Netherlands: Wageningen, 1974, pp. 20-22.

32. *Resettlement in Post-Revolutionary Ethiopia*.

33. *Ethiopia: Land Evaluation, Crop Environmental Requirement*, Technical Report, Part Three, The United Nations Food and Agricultural Organization of the United Nations, Rome, 1983, pp. 24-36.

34. Data obtained at Ekuna Kijang and Baro Abol settlement villages in Gambela. These figures are also cited by unofficial report written by the Ministry of Agriculture Office in Metu, Illubabor.

35. Ministry of Agriculture Zonal Office for Western Ethiopia, *A Study of Low-Cost Resettlement*, p. 43.

36. *Resettlement in Post-Revolutionary Ethiopia*.

37. Pankhurst, "Resettlement in Ethiopia."

6

Preventing Famine and Preserving the Environment: A Policy Approach

At the core of environmental degradation in Ethiopia are the forces that influence the management and utilization of land by peasant farmers. The intensification of pressure on the land, leading to accelerated erosion, is the primary cause of land degradation in Ethiopia. The massive amount of soil erosion in famine-prone regions of the highlands, mainly due to the excessive exploitation of the land by overgrazing, overcultivation, and deforestation, destroys the vegetative cover and reduces soil depth and quality. This destruction severely diminishes soil fertility and increases the chance of crop failure and vulnerability to famine.

Ending this spiral is the key to any viable strategy for the sustainable development of the Ethiopian highlands. Such a development strategy would require the formulation at the government level of policies and legislation conducive to peasant participation in conservation projects and appropriate technical packages at the local level that are geared to conservation and meeting the basic necessities of peasant households. In this regard, "conservation-based development" recommended by the Ethiopian Highland Reclamation Study, would be valuable because it centers on ways to reduce soil loss without taking land out of production.[1]

Conservation-based development is similar to the concept of sustainable development, whose main objective is to reduce poverty by providing livelihoods that minimize resource depletion and environmental degradation.[2] According to the Ethiopian Highland Reclamation Study, conservation-based development is to be attained primarily by increasing the vegetative cover to improve the quality of the soil by protecting it from erosion and to increase food production simultaneously.[3] The reclamation study stresses improved farming practices as a major means of keeping more vegetative cover on croplands. These include shortened land preparation and planting (less intensive land use), quick maturing plants, multiple cropping, closer spacing, forage cropping on fallow land, strip cropping, and planting crops requiring intensive cultivation on land less vulnerable to erosion.[4]

The reclamation study does not attribute any significant role to livestock population size and grazing patterns in the denudation of vegetative cover. Crop residue, which helps to reduce the impact of rain and to maintain moisture on croplands during the dry season, is effectively removed by livestock. Moreover, in spite of the recommended vegetative measures, the emphasis of conservation activities has been fundamentally structural, such as building terraces, various types of soil bunds, and check dams. These measures involve a great deal of earth moving (causing soil disturbance), take up productive land (particularly graded bunding), and are relatively costly. Structural measures are also plagued by the problems of poor maintenance and are not effective due to lack of participation by peasants, who resent giving up the land they would have for cropping or livestock grazing.

The Ministry of Agriculture policy in dealing with famine has been mainly directed at bringing an immediate increase in food production through a substantial investment of resources in a few selected "surplus-producing" weredas. Peasant agriculture is fundamentally rainfed in Ethiopia. The technical packages of surplus-producing weredas, which emphasize the provision of inputs such as fertilizer and improved seed, are largely inappropriate in areas such as Wollo, where there is a high variability in rainfall pattern often resulting in drought. The concentration of manpower and services in surplus-producing weredas has also inadvertently undermined the urgent task of ending the vicious spiral that has produced severe ecological imbalance in most parts of Wollo. The extension service requires a major reorientation in the training and placement of extension agents working in such famine-prone regions. It should focus on disseminating and demonstrating better farming, livestock, and forest management that would arrest environmental degradation.

The Ethiopian government does not have a population control policy at present. This is not to suggest that the government is against family planning or birth control, but rather that there is no concerted effort to control effectively the high population growth rate. The government does not feel that population is an urgent problem needing its attention. However, the Central Statistics Office, has clearly articulated the danger of population expansion to Ethiopia's economy. With its present high growth rate, Ethiopia's population will be 114.5 million by the year 2015, and even with effective population control, the population would still grow to 104.1 million people.[5] This growth is likely to result in an absolute shortage of land in most of the highland areas, and an enormous strain on health, education, and other social services. In many parts of Wollo, the increasing population has resulted in diminishing land size (below the minimal one hectare required to sustain peasant farming in most of the highland areas), overcultivation, the absence of fallowing, the cultivation of marginal lands, the shortage of fuelwood, and the conversion of dung into fuel. The net effect is a substantial reduction in soil fertility. In the case of Wollo, large family size, with a high number of dependent children, has meant less food reserve.

The primary reason for the unpopular resettlement program is to reduce human pressure on the land. Yet a preliminary study has shown that the population growth of settlers in settlement areas is reported to be higher (4% growth in some large-scale settlements) than in the rest of Ethiopia. Resettlement can temporarily reduce population pressure on degraded land. It cannot, however, be a substitute for an effective population control policy, which is the only viable solution for arresting land degradation. The high population growth rate also increases the demand for fuelwood, greatly contributing to the acceleration of deforestation. The prospect of controlling population growth in Ethiopia in the next two decades is fairly good provided that the government makes a concerted effort towards this objective. Rural women are organized into women's associations, which every peasant association is required to establish following the 1975 Agrarian Reform. Women's associations provide the institutional infrastructure at the village level to effectively disseminate family planning practices.

There is no coherent national forestry policy in Ethiopia, a lack that has significantly contributed to the depletion of forest resources and the impediment of afforestation activities. The demand for fuelwood is twice the supply—a major reason for deforestation. The only way to address this imbalance is by a substantial increase in wood supply, since lowering population growth on the demand side would require at least a twenty-year lag, even with effective population control. Trees around the homestead are the principal source of energy supply for peasant households. Yet, the absence of clear guidelines regarding tree ownership has resulted in insecurity, which has become a major obstacle to increasing wood supply at the village level.

The government afforestation effort is concentrated on promoting communal ventures, particularly in community forests. Peasants' attitudes towards community forest is clearly negative. They equate community forests with the government-owned state forests and only invest the minimum amount of work they are ordered to do by the peasant association. Thus, community forests under the present management will not be a major source of the wood supply urgently needed by peasant households. Peasants clearly prefer individual ventures in tree planting. Trees planted by individuals around their homestead and farm hold the most promise for a dramatic increase in wood supply. Tree planting is not only a technical problem but equally a political one. Suffice it to say, an effective national forestry policy depends on instituting appropriate incentive mechanisms and on taking full account of peasant preference for individual ventures in tree planting.

There is no clear policy regarding the utilization of trees planted around the gullies and wasteland, in community forests, and in hillside closures. The government campaign is exclusively directed towards planting more trees and protecting them, and there is hardly any mention of the benefits that peasants could acquire from the afforestation projects. Trees do not have ornamental value to peasant households. Government orders and peasant association campaigns may succeed in planting millions of trees but they do not secure their survival, which is very low, particularly in community forests. Tree planting and its protection would require the missing incentive for individuals and groups of farmers to utilize trees.

Entitlement to the utilization of trees grown on unproductive land could address the urgent need for increasing wood supply and arresting land degradation. In fact, unproductive land in the peasant association should be leased to individual peasant farmers who are willing to plant trees, and the benefits from the trees should be guaranteed to the farmers. This is likely to be more effective than government-sponsored large-scale tree plantations in restoring ecological balance. Thus, a national forestry policy that would guarantee tree ownership and utilization by individual farmers is the most viable strategy to overcome the socioeconomic constraints facing afforestation and conservation efforts in Ethiopia.

There is also no clear aim of afforestation activities. The needs of industry and urban and rural households are different, and appropriate means have to be designed to meet these varying needs. For example, if the objective is to increase fuelwood supplies among peasant households, then legislation that promotes tree planting around the homestead is vital. On the other hand, if the objective is to arrest erosion and degradation on hilly areas, then natural regeneration through a well-managed closure would be important. The lack of specifying the aim of afforestation projects has been underscored as a major constraint by Martin Bendz, an advisor on forestry to the Red Cross-funded Upper Mille and Cheleka Catchments Disaster Prevention Program in Wollo. Bendz emphasizes that clarifying the aim of forestry activities would greatly contribute to the selection of the best measure, the improvement of its management, and the selection of appropriate tree species for differing objectives.[6]

There is no government policy regarding livestock density or managing grazing land, both of which have a major role in land degradation. To be sure, such a policy would have to strike a balance between limiting the overall number of livestock maintaining essential ones, particularly oxen. Livestock are one of the most significant means of capital accumulation in rural Ethiopia, as they are free from any form of taxation. They are also a quickly disposable asset that enhances the availability of food reserve in the early stages of famine. The overwhelming emphasis on livestock improvement, which has been in the promotion of veterinary services, inadvertently contributes to livestock density rather than to the quality of livestock. Hence, it is central to improve the quality of livestock without increasing their numbers, a goal that is best attained by improving livestock feed. Neither the technical package of conservation projects nor livestock policies makes adequate attempt to deal with this problem.

One of the major conservation programs—hillside closure—has underestimated the role of livestock and livestock grazing in the process of degradation.

Peasant attitudes towards hillside closure have been mostly negative (particularly in communities that do not practice "cut and carry"), as it has meant the
accumulation of more grazing land by the government, creating serious shortage
for livestock grazing in their communities. Hillside closure has resulted in quick
natural regeneration on degraded hills that are under quarantine while it has
inadvertently created immense livestock pressure on productive land, exposing
it to severe degradation. Hence, it is vitally important for hillside closure to
introduce appropriate technical packages, such as suitable fodder trees, quick
growing grasses and legumes, and controlled pasture management where
peasants could harvest grasses and livestock feed. These packages would enable
farmers to overcome the severe shortage of grazing land and livestock feed and
could significantly contribute to the effectiveness of hillside closure in
rehabilitating degraded land.

The conservation policies in Ethiopia put great emphasis on cropping and
cropland and little on grazing and grazing land. Cropland may have more loss
of vegetative cover and may suffer more extreme erosion than grazing land, but
grazing land, which accounts for 51% of the total land cover as opposed to 13%
for cropland, contributes more significantly to soil loss in Ethiopia. Moreover,
the loss of vegetative cover on cropland is not exclusively due to cropping.
During the major rainy season, livestock graze on the slopes. Their role in the
denudation of the vegetative cover and in the "downstream effect," in which
soil is irreversibly lost, is greatly underestimated.

Furthermore, during the long dry season—nearly six months—cropland,
whether on the upper slope or valley bottom, is left open for unrestricted grazing.
Livestock feed on crop residue and vegetation, reducing the biomass cover and
causing soil crusting, which reduces soil fertility and increases the erosion level.
This again points to the major role of livestock and improper management of
grazing land in the loss of vegetative cover and productive land in Ethiopia. To
arrest this, it is important to seek policies that would substitute for livestock—a
major source of capital accumulation among peasant households—trees and tree
products, which would increase vegetative and biomass cover. Again this would
require a national forestry policy that would provide proper incentive to individual tree and land ownership.

At the heart of the government resettlement program is helping the "environmental refugees" from the famine-prone regions such as Wollo to be food
self-sufficient in the relatively fertile region of southwestern Ethiopia. Yet the
resettlement program has neither reduced the extraordinary pressure exerted on
degraded land nor made the peasants food self-sufficient in their new homes.
On the contrary, the peasants' fear of being forced to resettle has become a major
impediment to conservation and rehabilitation activities in Wollo.

The findings from settlement areas are deeply disturbing. Large-scale
settlements are highly mechanized and rely on heavy government subsidies to
keep up their operations. The government is secretive about this fact, because

admitting the provision of such a high level of food assistance would undermine the justification for the resettlement program. One of the major impediments to self-sufficiency in low-cost and large-scale schemes is the collective form of agriculture, which is deeply resented by peasants. Even the unofficial documents written by the Ministry of Agriculture staff recommend that the allocation of more land to individual farmers and less emphasis on the collectives are the only way out of the present agricultural debacle in the resettlement areas.

Above all, resettlement has posed an ominous environmental threat in the settlement areas themselves. Southwestern Ethiopia, where well over half of the country's natural forests remain, is experiencing a dramatic decline in its forest reserves and vegetation. Settlement sites, which were often selected with total disregard for the land quality and potential for long-term development, have suffered a devastating impact on their environment as well as on food production. Land that is under dense forest is more vulnerable to erosion when the forest and vegetative cover are removed. With the present high population growth rate and farming practices, any more massive settlements, such as the government intends, will lead to the expansion of cultivable land, intensive cultivation, less fallowing, and the drastic decline of forest resources. This would result in a substantial loss of soil fertility and the recreation of the conditions for more "environmental refugees."

One of the most important lessons gained from the resettlement scheme is the discovery that land where forests flourish is not necessarily the ideal environment for crop cultivation. An example of this is the experience in the Gilo Valley in Gambela and in the Dedesa Valley in Keffa, in which the soil had serious drainage problems after massive amounts of forest land were cleared. Some parts of Ilubabor and Keffa could specialize in forest and the forest products that would be a viable option for income generation and self-sufficiency of rural households in these regions. Again, this would call for a national forestry policy that would give adequate incentive for individuals, groups, and communities to invest in trees and tree products.

The greatest drawback of the resettlement program is its top-down approach, in which there is no involvement of peasant institutions and leaders. This lack of participation among peasants and peasant associations was also observed regarding the management and utilization of community forests and hillside closures. As a result, peasants have a negative attitude towards these conservation programs, from which they think they are unlikely to receive any benefit.

The villagization program, which presents a colossal environmental threat to peasant farming, also suffers from the top-down approach and from a total lack of participation by peasant institutions. Initiated throughout Ethiopia in 1985, the villagization program is based on the assumption that the settlement pattern of scattered homesteads is a fundamental hindrance to agricultural and socioeconomic progress.[7] This assumption is flawed. The premise behind villagization is best revealed by one of the government slogans (in Amharic) to promote villagization. Translated into English, it reads: "Today's villages are tomorrow's towns." In an industrialized society, economic development is distinctly associated with the concentration of people in towns and reduced human pressure on agricultural land. In a peasant dominated agrarian society like Ethiopia, such a concentration of people through villagization, without the resource base for industrialization, would mean an increased pressure on land resulting in degradation and a substantial decline in farming efficiency.[8] In Ethiopia, the highest leaders and party officials envision villagization as a short-cut in the formation of towns, which is to spearhead the development of the rural sector. Under the villagization program, peasants are required to dismantle their huts, abandon their homesteads, and build houses in a hastily selected place. The houses are built in closer proximity to one another and along straight lines similar to those of a town. As of March 1988, the government announced that nine million people moved into villages, in twelve regions excluding Tigraye and Eritrea.[9]

In Wollo, the number of farm families under villagization was less than 2%, the smallest percentage in all regions. In this sample, 93% of the interviewed farmers indicated that they would not like to move into the villages. Of those, the majority (41%) asserted that they could not afford to build new houses because of chronic shortages of wood and construction materials and the enormous demand on labor. In communities where there is a tradition of building stone houses, which last for generations, peasants find it outrageous to dismantle their stone houses and build thatched-roof huts, at their own expense.

The second largest group of farmers who did not want to relocate in new villages (24%) claimed that they were satisfied with their present homestead, which was already a village, and saw no reason to destroy their ancestral villages and move into another one. In our observation, the only difference between the existing villages and new ones built under the villagization program was that the houses in new villages were in a straight line. The third largest group (14%) reported that there was a serious shortage of land around the homesteads of those who lived in the new villages. This would greatly restrict or eliminate their ability to grow food crops and permanent cash crops on which they rely in times of famine. The fourth largest group (7%) indicated that a serious shortage of grazing land would result in new villages. The other reasons cited were that the farms would be further from their homes, restricting them from protecting their crops from birds and wild animals as well as from maintaining their fertility (5%); that the villages were crowded and would be vulnerable to disease (3%); that they would be subject to fire because of the thatched roofs built close to one another (3%); that the valleys where they would be asked to build their houses would be waterlogged and dangerous places to live (2%); and that they might have difficulty in getting along with people (1%).

This top-down approach has resulted in the inflexibility of the villagization program, which has become both too costly for the peasants and the government and disruptive of agricultural production and the environment. For example, Alemayehu Lirenso's field study on villagization showed that there must be different criteria when moving peasants into new villages in permanent crop growing areas and those involved in nonfarming activity such as pottery.[10] The process of villagization could have been undertaken gradually, smoothly, and at less cost by peasant associations, but only when they found it in their best interest. Peasant opposition to move into new villages provides the most convincing reason why the government should have only a facilitating role, at best, and leave the process of villagization to the peasantry. A decentralized approach to villagization, which peasants and their institutions undertake when they find it appropriate and at their own pace, could have offered some of the merits of villagization, such as providing social services at low cost.

The promotion of producer cooperatives (collective form of production) has also used the top-down approach, with a disproportionate amount of the Ministry of Agriculture's financial, human, and technical resources devoted to attaining this objective. There were also cases in Wollo where individual farmers were required to assist members of producer cooperatives without sharing any of their benefits. Wereilu Awraja, for instance, has the largest number of producer cooperatives in Wollo and the government sees it as a model for other awrajas. During the fieldwork, most of the producer cooperatives in the fertile valleys in Wereilu Wereda had not yet harvested their crops late in the dry season whereas most of the individual farmers had completed this task. The awraja party officials passed orders to the Ministry of Agriculture staff to mobilize individual farmers to help in harvesting the producer cooperative's crops fearing that they would be spoiled by the short rain season due any time. Individual farmers were often ordered to help in ploughing cooperative land, as the members were not able to complete the preparation of land for planting during the critical rainy season. Such labor contribution without remuneration is clearly in violation of the Ethiopian constitution.

There were also instances where the party intervened in a heavy-handed way to prevent the dismantling of producer cooperatives, against the wish of the members. In three producer cooperatives in Yeju Awraja (Anova and Gedobere in Gubalafto Wereda and Werekelo in Habru Wereda), all the peasant associations were converted into producer cooperatives. These cooperatives achieved the government's ultimate objective of the stage-by-stage transformation of peasant associations into producer cooperatives. A large number of farmers wished to leave the Werekelo producer cooperative because of their disenchantment with the management following the 1984 famine. To preserve the image of a successful producer cooperative, party officials and security forces intervened to intimidate the peasants who wanted to leave the cooperative. The guidelines for producer cooperatives clearly state that peasants should join voluntarily and coercion should not be used.

Due to the "Marxist" orientation of the Ethiopian government, the producer

The unpopular villagization program: Villages occupying the best agricultural land in the valley, Kutaber.

The government's "ideal" villagization scheme, Gerado, Dessie.

cooperative movement is administered centrally with little regard for peasants' interests. In most of the places covered under this study in Wollo, government policy ensured the allocation of the most fertile land to members of producer cooperatives. Land shortage, a serious impediment to increasing food production among individual farmers, is not the case in producer cooperatives which have more fertile land and few members. Yet, extension agents candidly express that they are plagued with low productivity. A policy that would enable the utilization of this productive land by the appropriate incentive mechanism to individual farmers could bring a dramatic increase in food production.

The most appropriate policy would be to let the cooperatives flourish or perish on their own merits. That is to say, peasants should be left alone to form producer cooperatives or dismantle them if it is in their interest to do so. If peasants had a free choice about whether or not to join producer cooperatives, the prospect of the movement would be bleak. Even those who are members of producer cooperatives are likely to dismantle collective's modes of farming for individual farming, provided that there is no government intervention. But, supporting the producer cooperative movement, mainly for ideological reasons, is costly for the government; the heavy investment, particularly at the expense of individual farmers, undermines its own effort in attaining food self-sufficiency.

Similarly, the Ethiopian government should delegate to peasant associations more authority over resettlement, and should limit its own role and the role of the party to merely facilitating those who would voluntarily like to resettle. Above all, priority should be given not to investing Ethiopia's meager resources in resettlement, but rather to reducing the root causes that have necessitated it to begin with. The most crucial steps towards attaining this goal depend on undertaking conservation activities and promoting projects that reduce vulnerability to famine by controlling the microenvironments at the community level. The findings from this study highlight that small irrigation schemes and agroforestry projects should occupy a central role in the attempt to attain food self-sufficiency and restore ecological balance in the highly degraded Ethiopian highlands.

Indigenous gravitational irrigation schemes involving the diversion of streams and rivers have played an indisputable role in reducing vulnerability to famine in Wollo. Labor, a major input of this system, is plentiful, and the streams that feed the major tributaries of the Nile originate in the highlands of Wollo. In spite of this, only 1% of the land is irrigated and the government effort is concentrated on building huge and expensive dams, with little success. For example, at the height of the 1984 famine in Wollo, officials of the Ethiopian government ordered the construction of the Borkena Dam, a large-scale irrigation project in Kalu Awraja (near Kombolcha) with no consultation with the Ministry of Agriculture, which has the technical capacity to evaluate such a project and has the ultimate responsibility for its operation. This irrigation project aimed to establish large-scale farms in the fertile Borkena valley to assist in the prevention of future famine. The scheme was plagued with numerous problems, such as not finding a foundation for the dam, siltation, and cracking, even before the operation started. The government is secretive about the costs (which are estimated to be very high) and this project is still not completed.

Pump installation, another government irrigation scheme, is reported to be unreliable because of a chronic lack of spare parts and fuel. Yet, the highlands of Wollo, which have enormous potential for small-scale gravitational irrigation, are totally untapped. Many peasant associations in this study are located close to streams that are tributaries of the Nile. However, for gravitational irrigation to be a permanent source of water supply, there has to be afforestation and watershed management activities on these bare highlands. Trees help prevent springs from drying up and improve the holding capacity of ground water, which would rectify the lack of water during the dry season—the greatest problem faced by most gravitational schemes. Afforestation of the highlands would help to maintain an adequate supply of water for gravitational irrigation schemes, as well as to stop massive loss of topsoil, which is the genesis of crop failure and famine in the Ethiopian highlands.

Agroforestry may be a trendy subject, but in highly degraded regions such as Wollo it is the essence of long-term development. What makes agroforestry extremely relevant in the famine-prone Ethiopian highlands is that it can provide vegetative cover without taking land out of production. Farmers can grow perennials such as coffee, fruit trees, and even fuelwood (which they can use as a source of cash), while at the same time providing biomass cover that is needed to prevent erosion and maintain soil fertility through most of the year. Agroforestry could also play an important role in providing livestock feed, which is a major means of improving the livestock quality in Ethiopia. It would also provide vegetative cover and reduce the immense pressure exerted by livestock on cropland.

An impressive feature of agroforestry, in the few communities that practice it, is that different perennial crops can be cultivated appropriate to the ecological zone and the needs of the farmers or the community. The most exemplary agroforestry practice was that observed in Rike, where annual crops were cultivated on fields, perennials near homesteads, and forest reserves on the hilly slopes. Agroforestry in this case provides food, cash income (through coffee), fuelwood, and, above all, the biomass cover that provides moisture availability throughout most of the year. Rike also had relatively higher rainfall as well as better distribution in the last twenty years than most places at similar altitudes in Wollo. Hence, agroforestry is a mechanism in controlling the microenvironment in famine-prone areas such as Wollo, where nature is capricious and the rainfall pattern unpredictable.

The present inflexible villagization program presents a colossal obstacle to expanding the agroforestry practice and to improving the microenvironment at the village level, which could help reduce the peasants' vulnerability in times of drought. Outsiders understanding of the villagization program seems limited. Their opposition is mainly based on the dubious premise that villagization is primarily aimed to facilitate the promotion of collectivization. This view was fostered by one of the consultancy reports on villagization in the Arsi region, undertaken for the Swedish International Development Authority.[11] There was no special effort towards collectivization in any of the newly established villages we visited in Wollo. This was also confirmed by Alemayehu Lirenso's extensive field study on the impact of villagization in Hararghe (the government showcase as a model for villagization) and the Shewa region.[12] An American journalist's account in Hararghe region gives further evidence that land, on the whole, under villagization is not collectivized.[13]

That highly publicized report by outsiders was dismissed as a politically motivated report lacking empirical evidence and may have contributed, inadvertently, to undermine the position of Ethiopian officials, particularly in the Ministry of Agriculture, who were opposed to the pace and the implementation of villagization programs. No discussion on villagization with Ethiopian officials took place. Rather, the National Villagization Coordinating Committee gave strong directives for the swift implementation of villagization. Villagization is a policy that so fundamentally affects the farming system and the survival mechanism of the Ethiopian peasantry.

The environmental impact of villagization on the three peasant associations covered by this study (in Kalu, Ambassel, and Dessie Zurie awrajas) was devastating. Under the villagization guidelines, individuals could own plots ranging from 1,000 to 2,000 square meters. In reality, most of the villages we visited in Wollo had plots well below 500 square meters because of the severe shortage of land in highland zones. In particular, the individual plots around the homesteads specifically allocated for farming under villagization were small (less than 20 square meters). They were so small that the most important plots in securing food and cash crops, and an important mechanism to introduce agroforestry, were effectively destroyed by villagization. Lirenso's study of two peasant associations in Shewa region, where most rural household were moved into villages, showed that private plots in the new villages were reduced by 95% compared with the private compound in their previous homestead. Before villagization the average size of the private plot in the two peasant associations was 1,000 square meters.[14] This study also cautioned that even 1,000 to 2,000 square meters of individual plot (which only few villages had) could not sustain the development of a peasant economy.[15]

After just one year (between our first visit in December 1987 and our second visit in December 1988), there was severe land degradation in the new villages. The enormous pressure exerted by livestock on the small land around the homestead and village resulted in the formation of gullies. Farmers were not planting trees. As one peasant farmer put it, "There is little land to cultivate maize for my children, much less to plant trees." Villagizaton was an obstacle to the planting of trees around the homestead, which would help increase the urgently needed wood supply for peasant households; limited the planting of permanent crops such as *enset* and coffee, which would increase vegetative cover; and effectively destroyed the *guaro* (the most fertile plot in peasant farming), which has served as a risk averting mechanism in times of crop failure. It would seem prudent for donor agencies to emphasize this devastating environmental impact of the villagization program in their discussions with Ethiopian officials.

What is the prospect of villagization in Ethiopia? Villagization is one of the few programs that the party and top officials in Ethiopia consider a success, and they are proud of it. One-third of the rural population was villagized in four years. However, it is this momentum that is likely to bring the collapse of villagization. Most of the village sites were selected hastily on unsuitable lands, which resulted in considerable environmental stress. Within a decade the environmental degradation in the villages will be such that it will be impractical to sustain them.

Peasants also will be forced to move out of these villages. This is already happening. For example, the Kelo peasant association (02), Kalu Awraja, is on the border of southern Wollo and the northern Shewa region. After the establishment of new villages in the Kelo peasant association, peasants moved to neighboring Shewa region where villagization had not been introduced. Such movement away from villages to homesteads is likely to be widespread and beyond the control of the government.

The above are some of the major policy constraints under which any conservation program has to operate in Ethiopia. These policies also greatly discourage many donor agencies interested in Ethiopia, such as the European Economic Community and the Swedish International Development Authority, from undertaking any long-term projects. Also, the technical packages of many of the projects supported by donor agencies in Wollo lack the special emphasis of arresting the reinforcing spiral of environmental degradation and vulnerability to famine at the village level. One of the few exceptions is the approach taken by the Ethiopian Red Cross project in Wollo, the Upper Mille and Cheleka Catchment Disaster Prevention Program (UMCC-DPP), which is implemented through the Ministry of Agriculture. The issue here is not whether the UMCC-DPP is a success and others are not. Rather, it is whether its technical package and integrated approach are likely to be effective.

Launched in 1985, the UMCC-DPP project initially covered fifty-six peasant associations in Ambassel and Kalu awrajas. At the time of the study it included seventy-two peasant associations. Its major objective was to overcome the lack of vegetative cover and the poor natural water storage capacity, which it considers to be the principal reasons for the large-scale food deficit. This project, by establishing a relationship between vegetation, soils, ground water storage, and the recharge of springs and streams, tries to create an awareness that drought is not totally caused by external factors beyond individual efforts. The project components include community water resource development, improved crop production and livestock development, agricultural practice and food storage, land use management, reforestation (including agroforestry), and preventive community health.[16]

The Upper Mille and Cheleka catchment area was totally devastated by the 1984 famine and was a classic example of the severe erosion and deforestation of the highlands in Wollo. During a special field visit to the project area in February 1989, it became evident that some of the major causes of environmental degradation identified in this study were addressed by the technical packages of this project.[17]

1. Most of the mountains were under hillside closure and were regenerating quickly. A considerable number of farmers indicated using the grass from the hillside closure through the "cut and carry" system, and the deep resentment against area closure was not as evident as we found elsewhere.

2. Agroforestry was introduced by providing seedlings, such as *Sesbania acculeata*, that could be used as forage and which at the same time enrich the soil on marginal lands or around fences by nitrogen fixation. In some peasant associations, fruit trees, such as papaya, guava, and coffee, were planted around the homesteads providing an additional cash source for farmers.

3. Small-scale irrigation was established by diverting rivers and pumping water from nearby lakes (lakes Haik, Ardibo, and Galba) and earth dams and ponds were constructed (for reservoirs and irrigation) to increase the water supply for agriculture and human and animal consumption. Around Bati (Kalu Awraja), where many perished during the 1984 famine year, farmers were growing vegetables during the dry season through an irrigation scheme from the nearby lake. The sale of vegetables to the nearby towns provided them with cash income at a needed time.

4. Livestock were improved by introducing superior breeds of cows and providing better legumes and livestock feed at the village level.

The Ethiopian Red Cross points to the Bati Relief shelter, which had many famine victims in 1984 and is now a training center for farmers, as an example of its success.[18] Although it is an exaggeration to attribute all credit to the project, it is fair to say that the project has made major strides in arresting environmental degradation and reducing vulnerability to famine in the catchment areas. The project's partial success largely stems from linking conservation and rehabilitation activities with short-term benefits, which resulted in a fairly good acceptance among farmers in the catchment area. This strategy, recommended by the Ethiopian Highland Reclamation Study as "conservation-based development," is missing in many conservation projects. Yet the movement towards self-sufficiency in famine-prone regions rests exclusively on restoring the ecological balance without denying farmers the means of their survival.

This project has significant implications for the Ethiopian government and donor agencies in the development of the famine-prone Ethiopian highlands. Instead of a policy of concentrating resources in surplus-producing weredas, it would seem more appropriate to rehabilitate regions such as Wollo on a catchment basis. For example, the government effort in the Borkena valley concentrated on building large dams and promoting large-scale state and cooperative farms. Yet, their contribution to improving food production has been insignificant. Instead of concentrating on the development of the valley, it would be more appropriate to develop the whole Borkena catchment (including the highlands) using the approach taken by UMCC-DPP.

When all is said and done, the role of the Ethiopian government is central to ending the vicious spiral of environmental degradation and vulnerability to famine. This would require the enactment of specific policies and legislation that would bring the effective participation of peasants into this process. In addition, reducing vulnerability to famine and environmental degradation requires a long-term investment by peasants who should be convinced that these activities are in their best interest. This would require a decentralized approach to these programs that would elicit the participation of peasants and peasant institutions in the process. Ending the specter of famine in Ethiopia will fundamentally involve the rehabilitation of the famine-prone regions. This would require the appropriate technical packages in conservation projects, supporting policies, and political commitment of the government.

Notes

1. M. Constable and Members of the Ethiopian Highland Reclamation Study, *Development Strategy*, Working Paper 24, Ministry of Agriculture, Addis Ababa, May 1985, pp. 8-10.

2. Edward B. Barbier,"The Concept of Sustainable Economic Development," *Environmental Conservation*, Vol. 14, 1987, pp. 101-107.

3. Norman Hudson, *Soil Conservation*, Ithaca, N.Y.: Cornell University Press, p. 217. Vegetative measures reduce erosion and prevent the expansion of gullies. For example, a longitudinal study in West Africa has shown that soil loss in ten years (1953 to 1963) on a bare plot was 1,265.7 tons/hectare while soil erosion was 9.4 tons/hectare on a plot protected from the impact of raindrops by gauze.

4. Constable, et al., *Development Strategy*, pp. 19-48.

5. Central Statistical Authority, *Population Projection of Ethiopia: Total and Sectoral (1985-2035)*, Population Studies Serial No. 2, Addis Ababa, June 1988, p. 30.

6. This view was expressed by Marten Bendz in our discussion on the need for a national forestry policy while we were both involved in fieldwork in Wollo.

7. National Villagization Co-ordinating Committee, *Rural Transformation*,

Addis Ababa, 1987.

8. Goran Hyden's study in Tanzania shows similar environmental stress because of the concentration of people in new villages without change in the peasant mode of production. See *Beyond Ujamaa in Tanzania: Underdevelopment and an Uncaptured Peasantry*, Berkeley: University of California Press, 1980.

9. *The Ethiopian Herald*, March 27, 1988, p. 1.

10. Alemayehu Lirenso, *Villagization and Agricultural Production in Ethiopia: A Case Study of Two Regions*, Institute of Development Research, Addis Ababa University, October, 1989.

11. John M. Cohen and Nils-Ivar Isaksson, *Villagization in the Arsi Region of Ethiopia*, Rural Development Studies No. 19, Swedish University of Agricultural Sciences, Uppsala, February 1987.

12. Lirenson, *Villagization*.

13. Jane Perlez, The New York Times, September 12, 1989, p. A4.

14. Lirenso, *Villagization*.

15. Alemayehu Lirenso, "Villagization as a Tool for Rural Development in Ethiopia: Policy and Issues," Paper presented at workshop on Options in Rural Development in Ethiopia, Chr. Michelsen Institute, Bergen, Norway, July 1989.

16. The Ethiopian Red Cross Society, *Ethiopia, Upper Mille and Cheleka Catchments Disaster Prevention Program*, Volume IV, Summary and Recommendations, 1986, pp. 26-30. See also: Elizabeth Kassaye, *From Disaster Relief to Development: The Experience of the Ethiopian Red Cross*, Institute Henry-Dunant, 1987, p. 23. Ann K. Qualman, "Wollo Rehabilitation and Disaster Prevention Projects," in Marry B. Anderson and Peter J. Woodrow, *Rising from the Ashes: Development Strategies in Times of Disaster*, Boulder, Colo.: Westview Press, 1989.

17. This trip was undertaken with Ato Getahun Tebeje, director of the project, as our guide. A retired Ministry of Agriculture Official for Wollo region, Ato Getahun commands a great deal of respect among donor agencies and the Ministry of Agriculture. His leadership has contributed partly to the success of the project.

18. Kassaye, *From Disaster Relief to Development*, pp. 24-25.

Appendix 1: Questionnaire to Assess the Socioeconomic Dimension of Ecological Degradation and Its Linkage to Famine in Wollo Region

Household No:_____

Date:_____

Enumerator:_____

Size of Peasant Association (PA):_____

Number of Households in PA: _____

I. Household Location

1. Name of the Awraja   1._____
2. Name of the Wereda   2._____
3. Name of the Peasant Association   3._____
4. Type of agroecological zone   4._____
    1. highland
    2. medium altitude
    3. lowland
5. Distance from all-weather road   5._____hrs
6. Distance from the nearest school   6._____hrs
7. Distance from the nearest clinic   7._____hrs
8. Distance from the nearest market   8._____hrs

II. Background of Household

9. Sex of respondent   9._____
    1. male
    2. female
10. Civil status   10._____
    1. single
    2. married
    3. divorced
    4. widowed
11. If married, how many times   11._____
12. Religion of household   12._____
    1. Muslim
    2. Christian
    3. other
13. Ethnic origin of household   13._____
    1. Amhare
    2. Tigrie

     3. Oromo

     4. other

14. How many children (both dead and alive) did you have
    in all marriages?   14._____
15. How many children are still alive?   15._____
16. If any of your childeren died of famine, how many?   16._____
17. How many persons live in your house including your children?   17._____
18. Age of respondent   18._____
19. Age of members of the household

Age	No. of Members of household
0-5	_____
6-17	_____
18-60	_____
60 +	_____

20. Can you read and write?   20._____

     1. yes

     2. no

21. Can your spouse read and write?   21._____

     1. yes

     2. no

22. Are you sending your children to school?   22._____

     1. yes

     2. no

III. Indicators of Ecological Degradation and Peasants' Perceptions

A. Soil Fertility & Water Availability

23. What is the major occupation of the household?   23._____

     1. crop farming

     2. livestock

     3. mixed farming

     4. other

24. What is the total size of your landholding?   24._____ha
25. What is the total size of your cultivated land?   25._____ha
26. If you do not cultivate all your holding how do you use the
    major part of the rest of your holding?   26._____

     1. for grazing   _____ha

     2. for fallow land

     3. other

27. Did you inherit this farm?   27._____

     1. yes

     2. no

28. If no, when did you start farming this land?   28._____
29. Is your landholding all in one parcel?   29._____

     1. yes

     2. no

30. If no, how many plots do you have and what are the size of
    your three major plots?   30._____

Plot 1	Plot 2	Plot 3
(largest)	(2nd largest)	(3rd largest)

a. Size (ha)   _____ha   _____ha   _____ha

b. Is your main plot the most fertile one.?   b._____
    1. Yes
    2. No

31. Where is your main and the next two largest plots
    located?   _____plot 1 (largest)
                                             _____plot 2 (2nd larg.)
                                           _____plot 3 (3rd larg.)
    1. top of hill & upper slope
    2. middle slope
    3. lower slope
    4. valley
    5. plateau
    8. escarpment
    9. plain

32. Where is your house located?   32._____
    1. top of hill & upper slope
    2. middle slope
    3. lower slope
    4. valley
    5. plateau
    8. escarpment
    9. plain

33. Indicate the major crops you grow, and average normal year
    yields and their primary use?

Plots	Crops	Normal Yield	Primary Use	
			consumption	cash
Main plot	_____	_____qts	_____	_____
Plot 2	_____	_____qts	_____	_____
Plot 3	_____	_____qts	_____	_____

    a. Average Annual yield on main plot?   a._____%
    b. Do you practice crop rotation on your main plot?   b._____
        1. yes
        2. no

34. How do you view the level of erosion on your main plot, since
    you started farming?   34._____Plot 1
    1. very severe
    2. severe
    3. minor
    4. no problem
    5. not certain

35. Has the problem of erosion been with you   35._____
    1. prior to birth (heard it from parents)
    2. since childhood
    3. since marriage
    4. in recent years

36. Have you observed a decrease in soil depth?   36._____
    1. yes
    2. no
    3. not certain

37. If yes, what is the extent of stoniness on your main plot?   37._____
    1. a great deal

    2. considerable

    3. few

    4. none

    5. not certain

38. How serious is the decline in soil fertility, on your
main plot, since you started farming, with reference
to normal year (adequate rainfall)?   38._____

    1. very severe

    2. severe

    3. minor

    4. no problem

    5. not certain

39. Among your three major plots, are some plots more
affected by decline in soil fertility than others?   39._____

    1. yes

    2. no

40. If yes, which one?   40._____

    1. plot 1

    2. plot 2

    3. plot 3

41. What are the most important causes contributing to
decline in soil fertility, in order of importance?

    1._____

    2._____

    3._____

42. Have you received advice/assistance on how to
prevent soil erosion?   42._____

    1. yes

    2. no

43. Was this advice useful in preventing erosion?   43._____

    1. yes

    2. no

44. In the past five years, was *belg* rain adequate and timely?   44._____

    1. yes

    2. no

45. If no, which years were total failures (in Ethiopian calendar)? 45._____

    1. 1983/84   _____

    2. 1984/85   _____

    3. 1985/86   _____

    4. 1986/87   _____

    5. 1987/88   _____

46. In the past five years, was *meher* rain adequate and timely?   46._____

    1. yes

    2. no

47. If no, which years were total failures?   47._____

    1. 1983/84   _____

    2. 1984/85   _____

    3. 1985/86   _____

    4. 1986/87   _____

    5. 1987/88   _____

48. Where do you get water from?   48._____

    1. spring

2. well
3. river
4. pump
5. roof catchment
6. other

49. Who in the household has the major responsibility for
   fetching water?   49._____
   1. husband
   2. wife
   3. other

50. How far do you travel to get water?   50._____
           Dry season _____hrs.
           Rainy Season _____hrs

51. Since you started residing here your walking distance
   to get water   51._____
   1. has become farther
   2. has become nearer
   3. remained the same

52. If it is farther or nearer, was this change   52._____
   1. since childhood
   2. since marriage
   3. in recent years
   4. other

53. Do you use any irrigation scheme?   53._____
   1. yes
   2. no

54. Do you experience waterlogging on your land?   54._____
   1. yes
   2. no

55. If yes, on which plots?   55._____

B. Pasture:

56. Do you graze in different areas during the rainy and dry season?   56._____
   1. yes
   2. no

57. If no, where is your main grazing area, in both seasons?   57._____
   1. slope (top, middle & lower)
   2. valley
   3. plateau
   4. cropland
   5. other

58. Is this grazing area   58._____
   1. your own plot
   2. owned by the PA
   3. other

59. If you graze in different areas, where is your main grazing
   area during the rainy season?   59._____
   1. slope (top, middle & lower)
   2. valley
   3. plateau
   4. cropland
   5. other

60. Is this grazing area   60._____
    1. your own plot
    2. owned by the PA
    3. other
61. And which one is your main grazing area during the dry season?   61._____
    1. slope (top, middle & lower)
    2. valley
    3. plateau
    4. cropland
    5. other
62. Is this grazing area   62._____
    1. your own plot
    2. owned by the PA
    3. other
63. Do you face shortage of grazing land?   63._____
    1. yes
    2. no
64. If yes, during which season?   64._____
    1. rainy season
    2. dry season
    3. both rainy and dry seasons
65. Would you still face the same problem, if your stock is reduced by   65._____
    1. 3/4
    2. 1/2
    3. 1/4
    4. would not like it to be reduced
66. Does area closure exist in your PA?   66._____
    1. yes
    2. no
67. If yes, do you practice cut and carry?   67._____
    1. yes
    2. no
68. What is your opinion about area closure?   68._____
    1. postive, because _____
    2. negative, because _____
    3. indifferent
69. Do you consider a large livestock size   69._____
    1. advantageous
    _____(reason)
    2. disadvantageous
    _____(reason)
    3. both advantageous and disadvantageous
70. Have you received advice/assistance on pasture management?   70._____
    1. yes
    2. no
71. Was this advice useful?   71._____
    1. yes
    2. no

C. Role of Trees:
72. Do you plant trees?   72._____
    1. yes

2. no
73. If no, why not?   73._____
74. If yes is this
    1. a private initiative or a
    2. communal one
75. What do you use trees for, in order of importance?
    1._____
    2._____
    3._____
    4._____
    5._____
76. Is there natural forest in your community? (with some
    assessment of what constitutes natural forest in a particular
    community)   76._____
    1. yes
    2. no
77. If there are none, have you heard or remember when there
    was one?   77._____
    1. heard from parents that there was natural forest
    2. have seen it during childhood
    3. have seen it at the time of marraige
    4. have seen it in recent years
    5. other
78. What are the major causes for the disappearance of forest/trees
    in your community?   78._____
    a. bringing forest land into agriculture (intensive cultivation)
    b. human consumption for fuel and other necessities
    c. livestock grazing and fodder
    d. settlements
    e. other
79. Does the community have a village woodlot?   79._____
    1. yes
    2. no
80. What are your sources of fuel and in what proportion?
    1. fuel wood _____%
    2. dung _____%
    3. crop residue _____%
    4. other _____%
81. Is there a shortage of fuelwood in your community?   81._____
    1. yes
    2. no
82. How serious is this shortage?   82._____
    1. extremely serious shortage (no fuelwood)
    2. considerable shortage (3/4 shortage)
    3. minimal shortage (1/2 shortage)
    4. no shortage (always available)
83. Who in the household has the major responsibility for
    collecting the major fuel?   83._____
    1. husband
    2. wife
    3. children
84. What is the average time you take in collecting your major fuel? 84._____

85. How often do you collect your major fuel?   85._____
    1. several times a week
    2. once a week
    3. less than once a week
86. Do you buy fuel?   86._____
    1. yes
    2. no
87. If yes, what is it?
    1._____
    2._____
88. On the whole, how do you view trees?   88._____
    a. trees have more advantages (positive)
    b. trees have more disadvantages (negative)
    c. have no opinion
89. Is there a tree planting program in your community?   89._____
    1. yes
    2. no
90. Of the available tree species, which one do you prefer for fuel?   90._____
91. Of the available plants, which one do you prefer for forage?   91._____
92. Of the available plants, which one do you prefer for construction? 92._____

IV. Socioeconomic Forces

A. *Land Use and Tenure System:*
93. Were you a tenant before the Agrarian Reform?   93._____
    1. yes
    2. no
94. Have you brought new land into cultivation since the Agrarian
    Reform?   94._____
    1. yes
    2. no
95. On the whole, what do you think of the quality of your land on
    your main plot?   95._____
    1. very poor
    2. poor
    3. adequate
    4. fertile
96. Do you grow enough for family consumption on your farm
    during normal years?   96._____
    1. yes
    2. no
97. Do you feel secure that the land belongs to you?   97._____
    1. yes
    2. no
98. Would you prefer to remain on your land or resettle
    somewhere else?   98._____
    1. stay on present farm
    2. resettle
99. Give reasons for prefering to stay or resettle:
    1._____

2._____

3._____

100. Have you been told to form villages in your PA?   100._____
    1. yes
    2. no

101. Would you prefer   101._____
    1. to remain in your present homestead
    2. establish or move into villages

102. Give reasons for prefering to stay or establish villages:
    1._____
    2._____
    3._____

103. Would you like to join producer cooperatives?   103._____
    1. yes
    2. no

104. If yes, why, and if no, why not?
    1._____
    2._____
    3._____

105. What inputs do you use to maintain soil fertility?   105._____
    1. chemical fertilizer
    2. manure
    3. plant residue
    4. other

106. Indicate the number of cattle and other animals you own:
    ox _____
    cow _____
    heifer_____
    calf_____
    goat_____
    sheep _____
    equines_____

107. Do you have oxen to plough all your land?   107._____
    1. yes
    2. no

108. If no, how do you get access to oxen?   108._____
    1. hire
    2. oxen for labor exchange
    3. oxen sharing
    4. other

109. How much can you plough with your own stock?   109._____
    1. 3/4 of the land
    2. 1/2 of the land
    3. 1/4 of the land
    4. less than 1/4 of the land
    5. other (specify)

110. Do you have a labor shortage in operating your farm?   110._____
    1. yes
    2. no

111. If yes, at which season?   111._____
    1. harvest
    2. ploughing

3. weeding
4. other (specify)_____

B. Marketing and Distribution

112. What are the major crops you sell at the market
(in order of importance) during normal years?

Type of crop	quantity(qts)	highest price (preharvest)	lowest price (postharvest)
1._____	_____	_____birr	_____birr
2._____	_____	_____birr	_____birr
3._____	_____	_____birr	_____birr

113. What are the major crops you sell at the market (in order
of importance) during famine years?

Type of crop	quantity(qts)	highest price (preharvest)	lowest price (postharvest)
1._____	_____	_____birr	_____birr
2._____	_____	_____birr	_____birr
3._____	_____	_____birr	_____birr

114. During famine years, are you required to sell grain to the
Agricultural Marketing Corporation?   114._____
    1. yes
    2. no

115. If yes, which crops and in what quantity?

Type of Crop	Quantity	Price	
1._____	_____	_____birr	_____birr
2._____	_____	_____birr	_____birr
3._____	_____	_____birr	_____birr

116. What things do you sell before abandoning farming and seek relief?
_____(first and second thing)
_____(the last thing)

117. Indicate the type of tax, levies and contribution you pay and the amount:

Type of taxes/contribution	Amount
1._____	_____birr
2._____	_____birr
3._____	_____birr
4._____	_____birr
5._____	_____birr

118. Are you able to pay these taxes/contribution?   118._____
    1. yes
    2. no

119. If no, have you been in debt to pay these taxes and contribution? 119._____
    1. yes _____(reason)
    2. no

V. Adoptive Strategies to Famine:

120. How many major famines have you seen in your lifetime
(indicate the worst famine first)?   120._____
    1.____yr
    2.____yr
    3.____yr

121. Were you affected by the 1984/85 famine?   121._____
    1. yes
    2. no
122. Were your relatives or others in your PA affected by the
    1984/85 famine?   122._____
    1. yes
    2. no
123. Did you receive food assistance during the 1984/85 famine?   123._____
    1. yes
    2. no
124. If yes, was it through   124._____
    1. relief center
    2. food for work
    3. other (specify) _____
125. Did your relatives or others in your PA resettle
    elsewhere at that time?   125._____
    1. yes
    2. no
126. If yes, have you heard what has happened to them?   126._____
    1. yes _____(state)
    2. no.
127. Do you know of any one who has moved back after
    being resettled?   127._____
    1. yes _____(indicate where)
    2. no
128. Has the 1984/85 famine changed your behavior (practice)
    individually or that of your PA/SC collectively?   128._____
    1. yes
    2. no
129. If yes, what are these changes/measures (planting
    crops or trees, building storage, etc.)?
       individually   _____
       collectively (PA) _____
130. Do you have some reserve food at present?   130._____
    1. yes
    2. no
131. If yes, can it last until the coming harvest (*belg*)?   131._____
    1. yes
    2. no
132. If no, do you have some cash which can be used to buy food?   132._____
    1. yes
    2. no
133. If no, do you have some cattle or other assets which can be
    used to buy food?   133._____
    1. yes
    2. no
134. Are you receiving food assistance at present?   134._____
    1. yes
    2. no
135. If yes, what is it and how much?
    _____(type of food)
    _____(quantity)

136. You receive this assistance through   136.____
  1. relief center
  2. food for work
  3. other (specify) ____
137. Is your PA/SC taking measures in prepartion for this crisis? 137.____
  1. yes
  2. no
138. If yes, what are these measures?
  1._____
  2._____
  3._____
139. Are you aware if your PA/SC has any grain store? 139.____
  1. yes
  2. no
140. If yes, what are the contents and quantity?
  contents _____
  quantity _____
  * (This has to be checked physically)
141. Do you think that famine will always occur? 141.____
  1. yes
  2. no
142. What do you think are the three most important causes
  of famine, in order of importance?
  1._____
  2._____
  3._____

Appendix 2: Questionnaire to Assess the Conditions of Settlers in Wollo Settlement Areas

Household No: _____

Date: _____

Enumerator: _____

Size of Peasant Association (PA): _____

Number of Households in PA: _____

I. Present Household Location

1. Name of the Region   1._____
2. Name of the Awraja   2._____
3. Name of the Wereda   3._____
4. Name of the Peasant Association or Producer Cooperative   4._____
5. Type of agroecological zone   5._____
     1. highland
     2. medium altitude
     3. lowland
6. Distance from all-weather road   6._____
7. Distance from the nearest clinic   7._____
8. Distance from the nearest school   8._____
9. Distance from the nearest market   9._____
10. Average distance to get drinking water   10._____
11. Average distance to get fuel   11._____

II. Previous Household Location in Wollo

12. Name of the Region   12._____
13. Name of the Awraja   13._____
14. Name of the Wereda   14._____
15. Name of the Peasant Association or Producer Cooperative   15._____
16. Type of agroecological zone   16._____
     1. highland
     2. medium altitude
     3. lowland
17. Distance from all-weather road   17._____
18. Distance from the nearest clinic   18._____
19. Distance from the nearest school   19._____
20. Distance from the nearest market   20._____
21. Average distance to get drinking water   21._____
22. Average distance to get fuel   22._____

III. Background of Household:

23. Religion of household   23._____
    1. Muslim
    2. Christian
    3. other
24. Ethnic origin of household   24._____
    1. Amhare
    2. Tigrie
    3. Oromo
    4. Other (specify)
25. Can you read and write?   25._____
    1. yes
    2. no
26. How many children (both dead and alive) came with you
    to resettle?   26._____
27. If any of your children died since you came here, how many?   27._____
28. How many persons live in your house including yourself?   28._____
29. Age and relation of members of the household

Age	No. of Members	Relation
0-5	_____	_____
6-17	_____	_____
18-60	_____	_____
60+	_____	_____

30. From where did you come to resettle here?   30._____
    1. from relief center
    2. from own farm
    3. while going to market place
    4. while going to church
    5. other (specify)
31. Did all members of your family come to resettle with you?   31._____
    1. yes
    2. no
32. If no, how many are still in Wollo and what is their relationship
    to you?

No. of Members	Relation
_____	_____
_____	_____
_____	_____

33. Has any member of your family or others in your PA
    returned to Wollo?   33._____
    1. yes (if yes how many___•___ and
       why_____)
    2. no
34. Did you leave some important belongings when you
    moved to resettle?   34._____
    1. yes _____(explain)
    2. no
35. Has your or member of your family's health been seriously
    affected since you resettled here?   35._____
    1. yes _____(explain)
    2. no

36. If yes, did any of them die?   36._____
    1. yes
    2. no

IV. Comparison of Present and Previous Farming Conditions:
37. What is the total size of your present landholding?   37._____ha
38. Do you cultivate all your landholding?   38._____
    1. yes
    2. no
39. If you no, what do you use the major part of the rest of your
    holding for?   39._____ha
    1. for grazing
    2. for fallow land
    3. other
40. Is your present landholding   40._____
    1. larger than the one in Wollo
    (explain)_____
    2. smaller than the one in Wollo
    (explain)_____
    3. similar in size to the one in Wollo
41. Is your landholding all in one parcel?   41._____
    1. yes
    2. no (how many?)_____
42. Indicate the major crops you grow at present and in Wollo and
    their primary use:

Maj. Crop in Sett. Area	Maj. Crop in Wollo	Primary Use	
		consumption	cash
1. _____	_____	_____	_____
2. _____	_____	_____	_____
3. _____	_____	_____	_____

43. What do you consider the level of your produce from these major
    crops since you came to resettle?   43._____
    1. more than adequate for family consumption
    2. just adequate
    3. not adequate
44. If it is adequate or more than adequate, what has contributed to it? 44._____
    1. fertile soil
    2. adequate rain
    3. availability of more land
    4. application of fertilizer/improved seed
    5. other (specify) _____
45. If you are not producing adequate food for your family consumption,
    what are your major reasons?   45._____
    1. _____
    2. _____
    3. _____
46. Were you able to produce enough for your family consumption when
    you were in Wollo, in normal years?   46._____
    1. yes
    2. no

47. Do you have more income or produce from your new farm than the one
     in Wollo?   47._____
         1. yes_____(explain)
         2. no _____(explain)
48. What is the single most important reason for your being resettled
     on your present farm?   48._____
         1. was deeply affected by 84/85 famine and had no alternative at that time
         2. ordered by the government to resettle
         3. unable to support family and was willing to resettle
         4. serious shortage of land
         5. poor quality of land
         6. other (specify) _____
49. Were you informed that you will receive government support if
     you resettled?   49._____
         1. yes
         2. no
50. Has this support been forthcoming?   50._____
         1. yes _____(explain)
         2. no_____(explain)
51. Do you plant trees at present?   51._____
         1. yes (how many since you resettled?)_____
         2. no
52. If no, why not?_____
53. Is there a tree planting program in your PA?   53._____
         1. yes
         2. no
54. If yes, is this planting for   54._____
         1. state forest
         2. community forest in the PA
         3. other
55. What are your sources of fuel and in what proportion?   55._____
                       Now   Wollo
         1. fuelwood   ____%   ____%
         2. dung   ____%   ____%
         3. crop residue ____%   ____%
56. Is there a shortage of fuel wood in your PA?   56._____
         1. yes
         2. no
57. Are you a member of a producer cooperative (PC) now?   57._____
         1. yes
         2. no
58. If yes, did you   58._____
         1. join voluntarily
         2. have to join (already a PC)
         3. other (specify)
59. Were you a member of a PC in Wollo?   59._____
         1. yes
         2. no
60. If you are not a member of a PC, would you like to join a
     producer cooperative?   60._____
         1. yes _____(reason)
         2. no _____(reason)

61. Do you feel at home in your present farm?   61._____
   1. yes
   2. no _____(explain)
62. Do you plan to continue living here or return to Wollo
   if possible?   62._____
   1. stay here
   2. would prefer to return to Wollo
63. What are the most important problems you and other
   settlers face in your PA?   63._____
   1. _____
   2. _____
   3. _____

Index

About the Book and the Author

Identifying the political and socioeconomic forces that feed the cycle of environmental degradation and famine in Ethiopia—forces that are major impediments to sustainable agricultural development—this study provides a rare comparison of peasants' views and government policies on key environmental issues such as resettlement, villagization, collective farming, population growth, livestock density, and the various approaches to conservation and rehabilitation activities in famine-affected areas.

Alemneh Dejene's conclusions are based on a combination of survey data, an in-depth case study, and participant observation at the village level. These lead him to prescribe policies and legislation that will provide needed incentives to peasant farmers while eliminating development programs that are unpopular with those farmers and harmful to the environment.

Alemneh Dejene was a research fellow at the Energy and Environmental Policy Center, John F. Kennedy School of Government, Harvard University, while undertaking this study. He is currently working at the World Bank, Southern Africa Agriculture Division, on integrating environmental issues in a strategy for sustainable agricultural development.

151